COMMON CORE ACHIEVE

Mastering Essential Test Readiness Skills

TASC Test Exercise Book

SOCIAL STUDIES

D1316350

Mc
Graw
Hill
Education

Bothell, WA • Chicago, IL • Columbus, OH • New York, NY

MHEonline.com

Send all inquiries to:
McGraw-Hill Education
8787 Orion Place
Columbus, OH 43240

ISBN: 978-0-02-140585-5
MHID: 0-02-140585-9

Printed in the United States of America.

1 2 3 4 5 6 7 8 9 RHR 19 18 17 16 15 14

Table of Contents

Congratulations! If you are using this book, it means that you are taking a key step toward achieving an important new goal for yourself. You are preparing to take the TASC Test Assessing Secondary Completion™, one of the most important steps in the pathway toward career, educational, and lifelong well-being and success.

Common Core Achieve: Mastering Essential Test Readiness Skills is designed to help you learn or strengthen the skills you will need when you take the TASC test. The Social Studies Exercise Book provides you with additional practice of the key concepts, core skills, and core practices required for success on test day and beyond.

How to Use This Book

This book is designed to follow the same lesson structure as the Core Student Module. Each lesson in the Mathematics Exercise Book is broken down into the same sections as the core module, with a page or more devoted to the key concepts covered in each section. Each lesson contains at least one Test-Taking Tip, which will help you prepare for a test by giving you strategies for how to approach multiple choice questions, or tips for using charts, graphs, or other information to answer questions. At the back of this book, you will find the answer key for each lesson. The answer to each question is provided along with a rationale for why the answer is correct. If you get an answer incorrect, please return to the appropriate lesson and section in either the online or print Core Student Module to review the specific content.

About the TASC Test for Social Studies

The TASC test for Social Studies assesses across five content categories (approximate percentage of test questions in each category is shown in parenthesis): United States History (25%), World History (15%), Civics and Government (25%), Geography (15%), and Economics (20%). You will have 75 minutes to complete the test. Questions may require you to analyze historical documents, photographs, speeches, maps, and other information presented in charts or illustrations.

Questions are all multiple choice. As you work through the lessons in this book, you will practice answering the multiple choice question format. Each multiple-choice question contains four answer choices, of which there is only one correct answer. When answering a multiple-choice question, look for any possible answers that cannot be correct based on the information given. You may also see extraneous information in the question that is used in the answer choices. Identify and eliminate this information so you can focus on the relevant information to answer the question.

Strategies for Test Day

There are many things you should do to prepare for test day, including studying. Other ways to prepare you for the day of the test include preparing physically, arriving early, and recognizing certain strategies to help you succeed during the test. Some of these strategies are listed below.

- **Prepare physically.** Make sure you are rested both physically and mentally the day of the test. Eating a well-balanced meal will also help you concentrate while taking the test. Staying stress-free as much as possible on the day of the test will make you more likely to stay focused than when you are stressed.

- **Arrive early.** Arrive at the testing center at least 30 minutes before the beginning of the test. Give yourself enough time to get seated and situated in the room. Keep in mind that some testing centers will not admit you if you are late.

- **Think positively.** Studies have shown that a positive attitude can help with success, although studying helps even more.

- **Relax during the test.** Stretching and deep breathing can help you relax and refocus. Try doing this a few times during the test, especially if you feel frustrated, anxious, or confused.

- **Read the test directions carefully.** Make sure you understand what the directions are asking you to do and complete the activity appropriately. If you have any questions about the test, or how to answer a specific item type using the computer, ask before the beginning of the test.

- **Have a strategy for answering questions.** For each question, read the question promptly, identifying the most important information needed to answer the question. If necessary, reread the supporting information provided as well as the answer choices provided.

- **Don't spend a lot of time on difficult questions.** If you are unable to answer a question or are not confident in your answer, move on and come back to it later. If you are taking the paper and pencil version of the TASC test, mark your test booklet so you can easily find questions you have skipped. If you are taking the computer-based version of the TASC test, the testing software includes a tool that allows you to mark questions and move on to the next question. Answer easier questions first. If time permits at the end of the test, go back and review and answer questions you have marked. Regardless of whether you have skipped questions or not, try to finish with around 10–15 minutes left so you have time to check some of your answers.

- **Answer every question on the test.** If you do not know the answer, make your best guess. You will lose points leaving questions unanswered, but making a guess could possibly help you gain points.

Good luck with your studies, and remember: you are here because you have chosen to achieve important and exciting new goals for yourself. Every time you begin working within the materials, keep in mind that the skills you develop in *Common Core Achieve: Mastering Essential Test Readiness Skills* are not just important for passing the TASC test; they are keys to lifelong success.

This lesson will help you understand how governments vary among countries and identify documents that contributed to American democracy. Use it with Core Lesson 1.1 *Types of Modern and Historical Governments* to reinforce and apply your knowledge.

Key Concept

Governments within a state, country, or region are responsible for establishing order, providing security, and directing public affairs.

Core Skills & Practices

- Compare Ideas
- Analyze Ideas

Types of Government

Different types of government exist throughout the world at the local, state, and national levels.

Directions: Read the following questions and choose the best answer.

1. **Which definition fits the meaning of the term *oligarchy*?**
   - **A** a form of government in which all power rests with only one person
   - **B** a form of government in which power is inherited by a king or queen
   - **C** a form of government in which power rests with a small group of people
   - **D** a form of government in which citizens vote on all issues of government

2. **Which of these statements best explains the similarities between the United States legislature and the Canadian parliament?**
   - **F** Both are examples of direct democracy.
   - **G** Both contain representatives elected by citizens.
   - **H** Both contain a few members who hold most of the power.
   - **J** Both select the chief executive from the political party with the most seats.

3. **Which statement describes how a dictatorship differs from a constitutional monarchy?**
   - **A** Constitutional monarchs have ceremonial power, but dictators have absolute power.
   - **B** Constitutional monarchs seize power from someone else, but dictators inherit power.
   - **C** Constitutional monarchs hold power for short terms, but dictators hold power for life.
   - **D** Constitutional monarchs have legislative power, but dictators have ceremonial power.

4. **An autocratic government is best described as one in which**
   - **F** all power rests with only one person
   - **G** power is inherited by a king or queen
   - **H** citizens vote on all issues of government
   - **J** power rests with a small group of people

Directions: Read the excerpts. Then answer questions 5–8.

[B]ut an oligarchy and democracy differ in this from each other, in the poverty of those who govern in the one, and the riches of those who govern in the other; for when the government is in the hands of the rich, be they few or be they more, it is an oligarchy; when it is in the hands of the poor, it is a democracy: but, as we have already said, the one will be always few, the other numerous, but both will enjoy liberty; and from the claims of wealth and liberty will arise continual disputes with each other for the lead in public affairs.

—Aristotle in *A Treatise on Government*

Is it credible that the democracy which has annihilated the feudal system and vanquished kings will respect the citizen and the capitalist? Will it stop now that it has grown so strong and its adversaries so weak? None can say which way we are going, for all terms of comparison are wanting: the equality of conditions is more complete in the Christian countries of the present day than it has been at any time or in any part of the world; so that the extent of what already exists prevents us from foreseeing what may be yet to come.

—Alexis De Tocqueville in *Democracy in America*

5. **What are Aristotle and Tocqueville both concerned about regarding democracy?**
   A the strength of oligarchies
   B the poverty of those who govern
   C the liberty of Christian countries
   D the power of the rich versus the poor

6 **According to Aristotle, when is a democracy like an oligarchy?**
   F when those in power are poor
   G when those in power are wealthy
   H when those in power are in the majority
   J when those in power are in the minority

7. **What is Tocqueville worried about regarding the future of democracy?**
   A that democratic governments will overtake the world
   B that the feudal system will return to Christian nations
   C that monarchies will replace democratic governments
   D that citizens and capitalists will be treated relatively equally

8. **What does Aristotle most likely believe will be the source of ongoing disputes over leadership in the future?**
   F the presence of the poor
   G claims of both wealth and liberty
   H restrictions on liberty for the poor
   J restrictions on the amount of wealth held by one person

Documents That Contributed to the Development of American Democracy

Several historical documents played an important role in the establishment of the United States government.

Directions: Read the following questions and choose the best answer.

9. **The Declaration of Independence and the Virginia Declaration of Rights assert that**

   A all citizens should be given the right to worship as they choose

   B people have a duty to change a government that is not trustworthy

   C government draws its rightful power from the consent of the people

   D citizens must have a right and a means to acquire and own property

10. **Why was the Bill of Rights added to the Constitution in 1791?**

    F to convince the remaining states to ratify the Constitution

    G to ensure that the presidency does not become a monarchy

    H to guarantee that the rights of individual citizens are protected

    J to balance the power between the central government and the states

Directions: Read the excerpt below. Then answer questions 11–13.

Fifteenth Amendment—The right of citizens of the United States to vote shall not be denied or abridged by the United States or by any State on account of race, color, or previous condition of servitude.

Nineteenth Amendment—The right of citizens of the United States to vote shall not be denied or abridged by the United States or by any State on account of sex.

Twenty-Fourth Amendment—The right of citizens of the United States to vote in any primary or other election for President or Vice President, for electors for President or Vice President, or for Senator or Representative in Congress, shall not be denied or abridged by the United States or any State by reason of failure to pay any poll tax or other tax.

Twenty-Sixth Amendment—The right of citizens of the United States, who are eighteen years of age or older, to vote shall not be denied or abridged by the United States or by any State on account of age.

11. **The amendments to the United States Constitution are listed in numerical and chronological order. Based on this information, which of these is true? The right to vote was granted to**

    A African American men before women of any race

    B white women before African American men or women

    C eighteen-year-old women before eighteen-year-old men

    D African Americans before they were legally declared citizens

12. Many citizens who were old enough to serve in the military were angered that they were not old enough to vote. Their protests resulted in which amendment?

   F the Fifteenth Amendment

   G the Nineteenth Amendment

   H the Twenty-Sixth Amendment

   J the Twenty-Fourth Amendment

13. Which amendment made voting a right for those who were living in poverty?

   A the Fifteenth Amendment

   B the Nineteenth Amendment

   C the Twenty-Sixth Amendment

   D the Twenty-Fourth Amendment

Directions: Read the following questions and choose the best answer.

14. Read the sentence in the box.

> That to secure these rights, Governments are instituted among Men, deriving their just powers from the consent of the governed . . .

Which type of government does this statement describe?

   F democracy

   G dictatorship

   H monarchy

   J oligarchy

15. Like the Bill of Rights, the Magna Carta was written to

   A define the structure of the court system

   B protect the rights of individual citizens

   C define the structure of the government

   D protect the rights of those who rule

16. Including the Bill of Rights, there are 27 amendments. Based on this information, what conclusion can <u>best</u> be reached about the inclusion of an amendment process in the Constitution?

   F The authors of the Constitution could not agree on the rights to include.

   G The authors of the Constitution realized it was a flawed document that would require revision.

   H The amendment process was included because the authors did not want a Constitution that would be changed.

   J An amendment process was included so the Constitution would be a flexible document and change as society changed.

 **Test-Taking Tip**

When you are answering questions about a primary source passage, look for key words and facts within the question that you can then find within the passage.

This lesson will help you understand what led to the Constitutional Convention and how compromises led to constitutional amendments. Use it with Core Lesson 1.2 *American Constitutional Democracy* to reinforce and apply your knowledge.

Key Concept

The Constitution was not met with universal approval and had to be changed to get the new American states to approve it.

Core Skills & Practices

- Judge the Relevance of Information
- Read a Bar Graph

The Need for a Constitution

After the Revolutionary War, the colonists needed to establish a plan for creating a new central government. Each state created its state constitution, most of which included a "bill of rights." The first plan for a central government, the Articles of Confederation, was drawn up. However, it did not provide an executive officer, a national system of courts, or a way for the nation to collect taxes to pay for its war debts.

Directions: Read the following questions and choose the best answer.

1. **Why did the Articles of Confederation retain many important powers for the states rather than for the federal government?**
   A The states could not agree on the role the federal government should play.
   B The Framers of the Articles of Confederation wanted a government like that of Great Britain.
   C The states disagreed on how much power each state should have in the federal government.
   D The Framers of the Articles of Confederation worried that a strong federal government would abuse its power.

2. **Under *constitutionalism*, which of these is true?**
   F The government's power is unlimited.
   G The government's power comes from its citizens.
   H The government's power is based on a set of written rules.
   J Provisions for change within the government are unnecessary.

3. **Why did farmers take up arms against state governments during Shays's Rebellion?**
   A The farmers believed that the Articles of Confederation were unfair.
   B The state governments did not support the creation of a new constitution.
   C The courts and tax collectors had begun seizing farms as repayment for debt.
   D The farmers believed that the federal government had incurred too much debt.

A Nation Built on Compromise

The new government under the Articles of Confederation was not successful. The Constitutional Convention convened in 1787 to rewrite the rules by which the United States would work. The result was the United States Constitution.

Directions: Read the following questions. Then select the correct answer.

4. **Citizens retain popular sovereignty in a country by which of these methods?**

    F running for office

    G voting in federal, state, and local elections

    H paying taxes at the federal, state, and local levels

    J taking part in the judicial system as jurors at trials

5. **A president's ability to nominate federal judges is an example of**

    A checks and balances

    B limited government

    C popular sovereignty

    D judicial review

6. **What did the delegates to the Constitutional Convention include in the Constitution to address their concerns about being ruled by a strong central government?**

    F the Bill of Rights

    G a judicial branch

    H separation of powers

    J a way to amend the Constitution

7. **Which definition fits the meaning of the term *federalism*?**

    A a loose alliance of states

    B shared power between the states and a central government

    C the fair distribution of power between large and small states

    D a system in which each branch of government limits the power of the other two branches

 **Test-Taking Tip**

Don't get stuck on a difficult question. Instead, make a small mark next to the question. Go back and answer that question later. Other parts of the test may give you a clue that will help you answer that question.

Directions: Read the excerpt. Then answer questions 8 and 9.

Written by James Madison, [Federalist, No. 10] defended the form of federal government proposed by the Constitution. Critics of the Constitution argued that the proposed federal government was too large and would be unresponsive to the people.

In response, Madison explored majority rule v. minority rights in this essay. He countered that it was exactly the great number of factions and diversity that would avoid tyranny. Groups would be forced to negotiate and compromise among themselves, arriving at solutions that would respect the rights of minorities. Further, he argued that the large size of the country would actually make it more difficult for **factions** to gain control over others. "The influence of factious leaders may kindle a flame within their particular States, but will be unable to spread a general conflagration through the other States."

—The Bill of Rights Institute

8. **Based on the selection above, select the best definition for** *faction*.
   - **F** people who work for the government
   - **G** a controlling majority group in a country
   - **H** a leader who seeks to change the government
   - **J** a smaller group that disagrees with a larger group

9. **With which statement would Madison agree regarding majority rule and minority rights?**
   - **A** Liberty should not be limited in order to reduce the number of factions.
   - **B** Liberty should be limited in order to reduce the number of factions.
   - **C** Majority rule sometimes means minority rights will suffer.
   - **D** The government should build consensus on all issues.

Directions: Read the following question and choose the best answer.

10. **Which quote best describes the rule of law?**
   - **F** For as in absolute governments the King is law, so in free countries the law ought to be king; and there ought to be no other. —Thomas Paine
   - **G** A Bill of Rights is what the people are entitled to against every government, and what no just government should refuse. —Thomas Jefferson
   - **H** The fundamental law of the militia is, that it be created, directed and commanded by the laws, and ever for the support of the laws. —John Adams
   - **J** In framing a government which is to be administered by men over men you must first enable the government to control the governed. —James Madison

Amending the Constitution

The United States is governed according to the rules set forth in the Constitution. The Framers of the document created a way to amend—to change or add to—the Constitution through the passage of amendments.

Directions: Read the following questions and choose the best answer.

11. **The first four amendments of the Bill of Rights addressed which of these concerns held by the colonists?**

    A unfair court procedures

    B discrimination based on race

    C basic rights violated by Britain before the Revolutionary War

    D power held by the states not reserved for the central government

12. **Read the information in the box.**

    > The Second Amendment states: *A well regulated militia, being necessary to the security of a free state, the right of the people to keep and bear arms, shall not be infringed.*
    >
    > A survey was conducted by Gallup on January 14–16, 2011, in which people were asked their position on passing stronger gun laws. The survey results showed that 26% were **strongly in favor**, 23% were **in favor**, 23% were **opposed**, 27% were **strongly opposed**, and 2% had **no opinion.**

    What conclusion can you draw about the American public's position on gun laws from this Gallup poll?

    F Most people are in favor of stronger gun laws.

    G Most people are not in favor of stronger gun laws.

    H Americans are not interested in the issue of gun regulation.

    J Americans are divided over whether there should be stronger gun laws.

13. **Which two steps are required in the process of changing, or amending, the Constitution?**

    A proposing an amendment in Congress and ratifying the amendment by a majority of states

    B passing of the amendment in the House and then passing of the amendment in the Senate

    C passing of the amendment in Congress and then by a minority of states

    D ratifying the amendment and agreement by a majority of states

14. **What feature of the Constitution enables it to remain relevant?**

    F The Constitution provides for a strong central government.

    G The language used in the Constitution is simple and timeless.

    H The Constitution can be amended to address new or changing issues.

    J The Constitution is referred to on a continuing basis by government and the courts.

This lesson will help you understand the power of state and federal governments and how both are structured. Use it with Core Lesson 1.3 *Structure of American Government* to reinforce and apply your knowledge.

Key Concept

The federal and state governments provide services to people, but they have unique roles and responsibilities.

Core Skills & Practices

- Read a Chart
- Determine Central Ideas

The Three Branches of Government

The Framers of the United States Constitution created a new government that had a strong, but limited, central government divided into three branches—executive, legislative, and judicial—each with a specific set of powers.

Directions: Read the following questions and choose the best answer.

1. **Which is the primary job of the president?**

   A to sign or veto legislation

   B to act as commander-in-chief

   C to run the executive department

   D to entertain and inform foreign diplomats

2. **Read the information in the box.**

   > "I do solemnly swear (or affirm) that I will faithfully execute the Office of President of the United States, and will to the best of my Ability, preserve, protect and defend the Constitution of the United States." (Oath of Office of the President of the United States)

   Which part of the oath of office applies to the president's primary job?

   F I ... will faithfully execute the Office of President ...

   G I will ... preserve ... the Constitution ...

   H I will ... protect ... the Constitution ...

   J I will ... defend ... the Constitution ...

✔ Test-Taking Tip

During an exam, it often helps to take a momentary break, shut your eyes, and take a few deep breaths. It will help you clear your head and stay fresh during the exam session. Just two or three 30-second breaks can be very beneficial.

3. **Which is an example of checks and balances?**

A The Supreme Court reviews decisions made by lower courts.

B The president issues a pardon to someone who has been convicted of a crime.

C The Congress amends a law that the Supreme Court has found to be unconstitutional.

D The Secretary of Energy gives the president advice, but the president does not take it.

4. **Look at the chart.**

Division of Powers

Executive Branch	Legislative Branch	Judicial Branch
President	Congress	Supreme Court
• Enforces the laws • Acts as commander-in-chief of the armed forces • Appoints ambassadors, judges, and other officials • Makes treaties with other nations	• Writes the laws • Raises troops for armed forces • Decides how much money may be spent on government programs	• Interprets the laws • Reviews court decisions

Based on the chart, what powers are shared by the executive and legislative branches of government?

F commerce powers

G foreign policy powers

H military powers

J money powers

Directions: Read the excerpt. Then answer the questions 5 and 6.

To members of Congress, the president now looms large in the legislative process. He sets the national agenda and has behind him the vast knowledge and expertise of the federal bureaucracy. In this media-driven age, he speaks with one voice, as against the many of Congress, making it easier for him to command the attention of the cameras.

—Radio broadcast of Lee Hamilton, United States Representative to Congress from Indiana
(1965–1999)

5. **What has allowed the president to have a greater role in the legislative process?**

A the media

B former presidents

C members of Congress

D the federal bureaucracy

6. **What does Congressman Lee Hamilton imply about presidents prior to the 20th century?**

   F They did not cooperate with Congress.

   G They never used the media to communicate.

   H They were not supported by a federal bureaucracy.

   J They did not have as much influence on legislation.

The Power of State Government

States share some powers with the federal government, however some powers are held only by the states.

Directions: Read the excerpt. Then answer question 7.

McCulloch v. *Maryland* (1819)

In 1816 Congress established the Second National Bank to help control the amount of unregulated currency issued by state banks. Many states questioned the constitutionality of the national bank. Maryland set a precedent by requiring taxes on all banks not chartered by the state. In 1818 the State of Maryland approved legislation to impose taxes on the Second National Bank chartered by Congress.

James W. McCulloch, a federal cashier at the Baltimore branch of the [United States] bank, refused to pay the taxes imposed by the state. Maryland filed a suit against McCulloch in an effort to collect the taxes. The Supreme Court, however, decided that the chartering of a bank was an implied power of the Constitution, under the "elastic clause," which granted Congress the authority to "make all laws which shall be necessary and proper for carrying into execution" the work of the federal government.

. . . The proceedings posed two questions: Does the Constitution give Congress power to create a bank? And could individual states ban or tax the bank? The court decided that the federal government had the right and power to set up a federal bank and that states did not have the power to tax the federal government. Marshall ruled in favor of the federal government and concluded, "the power to tax involves the power to destroy."

7. **The power to set up a bank is shared by the state and federal governments. What is this shared power known as?**

   A equilateral power

   B concurrent power

   C a reserved power

   D an identical power

Directions: Read the following questions. Then select the best answers.

8. **Chief Justice Marshall included this statement in his decision in *McCulloch* v. *Maryland*: "The power to tax involves the power to destroy." What did Marshall mean by this statement?**

    F The power to tax is reserved for the federal government alone.

    G The "elastic clause" gives Congress a power that is at times destructive.

    H The Constitution does not recognize the state or federal government's right to tax.

    J The state governments could use the power to tax to weaken the federal government.

9. **Which was the judicial branch's original area of responsibility?**

    A cases that involved the appointment of judges at a state level

    B issues existing between the executive and legislative branches

    C cases between states and those involving heads of other nations

    D cases that involved issues between the Senate and House of Representatives

The Structure of State Government

State governments are organized similarly to the federal government with executive, legislative, and judicial branches.

Directions: Read the following questions. Then select the best answers.

10. **Which is the definition of the term *referendum*?**

    F a charge brought against a federal government official

    G the power to remove a public official by popular vote

    H a popular vote on a measure passed by a legislature

    J the power of a chief executive to overturn a law

11. **Like Congress, what do state legislatures have the power to do?**

    A declare war

    B borrow money

    C rule a law unconstitutional

    D regulate trade within a state

12. **If the governor of a state is equivalent to the president of the United States, which office would be equivalent to the vice president?**

    F attorney general

    G lieutenant governor

    H secretary of state

    J state auditor

13. **Which power is reserved for state and local government only?**

    A the power to levy taxes

    B the power to hold elections

    C the power to borrow money

    D the power to establish schools

This lesson will help you understand how civil rights have progressed for American citizens, particularly for African Americans and women. Use it with Core Lesson 2.1 *Individual Rights and Responsibilities* to reinforce and apply your knowledge.

Key Concept

Constitutional amendments and new laws have helped extend civil rights to more people in the United States.

Core Skills & Practices

- Identify Point of View
- Identify Cause-and-Effect Relationships

Civil Rights and Civil Liberties

Freedoms that are guaranteed by the Constitution are called civil liberties. Among them are freedom of speech, religion, and assembly. Civil rights are the rights of full citizenship and equality under the law. Citizens and aliens—noncitizens in the United States—are guaranteed these civil rights.

Directions: Read the following questions and choose the best answer.

1. **Look at the chart.**

Civil Liberties	Civil Rights
To vote in an election	To live wherever you choose
To speak your opinion	

Which of these is a civil right that could complete the table above?

A to assemble peacefully

B to practice the religion of your choice

C to be free from discrimination at work

D to be free from illegal searches and seizures

Test-Taking Tip

When using a chart, first read the title of the chart to find out the topic. Then read the row and column headings to see how the chart is organized. Finally, skim the information in the chart to see whether you can make any generalizations about it.

2. Read the information in the box.

> . . . in all capital or criminal prosecutions a man has a right to demand the cause and nature of his accusation, to be confronted with the accusers and witnesses, to call for evidence in his favor, and to a speedy trial by an impartial jury . . .
>
> —from *Virginia Declaration of Rights* (1776), by George Mason

George Mason's point of view regarding the rights of the accused is reflected in which Constitutional amendment?

F First Amendment

G Sixth Amendment

H Fourteenth Amendment

J Nineteenth Amendment

3. Read the information in the box.

> Congress shall make no law respecting an establishment of religion, or prohibiting the free exercise thereof; or abridging the freedom of speech, or of the press; or the right of the people peaceably to assemble, and to petition the Government for a redress of grievances.
>
> — First Amendment to the Constitution

How does the Establishment Clause of the First Amendment separate church and state?

A It allows the government to levy taxes against churches.

B It prevents the government from ruling on religious matters.

C It prevents the government from endorsing a particular religion.

D It allows the government to prosecute people who establish religions.

4. Read the information in the box.

> . . . the person in custody must, prior to interrogation, be clearly informed that he has the right to remain silent, and that anything the person says will be used against him in court; the person must be clearly informed that he has the right to consult with a lawyer and to have the lawyer with him during interrogation, and that, if he is indigent, a lawyer will be appointed to represent him.
>
> —Chief Justice Earl Warren, *Miranda* v. *Arizona* (1966)

The Warren Court most likely based its decision in *Miranda* v. *Arizona* on what Constitutional amendment?

F First Amendment

G Fifth Amendment

H Fourth Amendment

J Fifteenth Amendment

Civil Rights for African Americans

At the time the Constitution was written—and for many years thereafter—only white male property owners held the right to vote. The Civil War banned slavery in the United States and extended civil rights to all males born or naturalized in America. Those rights are guaranteed by the Thirteenth, Fourteenth, and Fifteenth Amendments.

Directions: Read the following questions and choose the best answers.

5. **What was the effect of poll taxes and literacy tests?**
   A African Americans were prevented from voting.
   B African Americans were prevented from owning property.
   C Noncitizens were prevented from practicing their religion.
   D Noncitizens were prevented from protesting against discrimination.

6. **What was the Supreme Court ruling in *Plessy* v. *Ferguson* (1896)?**
   F African Americans had the equal right to own land.
   G African Americans could not be kept from running for office.
   H Schools for African American children did not have to be built.
   J Segregation was legal as long as facilities were "separate but equal."

7. **Read the information in the box.**

   > Any law that degrades human personality is unjust. All segregation statutes are unjust because segregation distorts the soul and damages the personality. It gives the segregator a false sense of superiority and the segregated a false sense of inferiority.
   >
   > —Dr. Martin Luther King, Jr.

   Dr. King's point of view is most clearly reflected in
   A the Establishment Clause of the First Amendment
   B *Brown* v. *Board of Education, Topeka, Kansas*
   C the Equal Pay Act of 1963
   D *Plessy* v. *Ferguson*

Women's Rights

After the Civil War, the women who championed voting rights for African American men turned their attention toward securing the same rights for women. Their decades-long struggle was finally won with the passage of the Nineteenth Amendment (1920), which gave women the right to vote in national elections. In subsequent years, women's rights activists have secured additional protections against gender discrimination in the workplace and in higher education.

Directions: Read the following question and choose the best answer.

8. **Which definition fits the meaning of the term *suffrage*?**
   F right to vote
   G religious freedom
   H civil disobedience
   J separation of races

Directions: Study the timeline. Then answer questions 9 and 10.

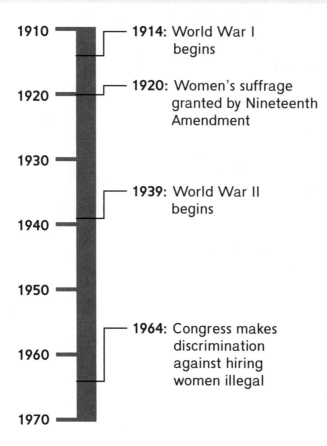

1910

1914: World War I begins

1920

1920: Women's suffrage granted by Nineteenth Amendment

1930

1939

1939: World War II begins

1940

1950

1964: Congress makes discrimination against hiring women illegal

1960

1970

9. **Based on this information, you can conclude that during and after World War II, women realized that they lacked equality with men in the area of**

   A employment rights

   B custody rights

   C property rights

   D voting rights

10. **Which best completes the timeline above?**

    F Women gain the right to vote in state elections.

    G Equal Rights Amendment ratified by the states.

    H Congress makes it illegal to pay men more than women for the same job.

    J A law is passed that guarantees women equal facilities in college athletics.

This lesson will help you understand the role of political parties in American politics and how interest groups and private individuals participate in our democratic society. Use it with Core Lesson 2.2 *Political Parties, Campaigns, and Elections* to reinforce and apply your knowledge.

Key Concept

People can make their views known and influence public policy through political parties and interest groups.

Core Skills & Practices

- Analyze Ideas
- Interpret Political Cartoons

American Political Parties

Political parties are organizations of like-minded individuals who work to influence national policies by nominating candidates for elected office.

Directions: Read the excerpt. Then answer questions 1 and 2.

. . . there is not a liberal America and a conservative America—there is the United States of America. There is not a black America and a white America and Latino America and Asian America; there's the United States of America. The pundits like to slice-and-dice our country into Red States and Blue States; Red States for Republicans, Blue States for Democrats. But I've got news for them, too. We worship an awesome God in the Blue States, and we don't like federal agents poking around in our libraries in the Red States. We coach Little League in the Blue States and have gay friends in the Red States. There are patriots who opposed the war in Iraq and there are patriots who supported it. We are one people, all of us pledging allegiance to the stars and stripes, all of us defending the United States of America.

—Senator Barack Obama, Keynote Address, 2004 Democratic National Convention

1. **In this speech, Senator Obama was most likely trying to appeal to which group of voters?**

   A   ethnic groups

   B   independent voters

   C   religious voters

   D   veterans groups

2. **Senator Obama gave this speech at his party's national convention. A national convention has two main tasks. Which one of these two tasks did Senator Obama's speech most likely achieve?**

   F   raising campaign funds

   G   nominating a candidate

   H   expressing a party's beliefs

   J   forming a coalition government

Directions: Look at the chart. Then answer questions 3–5.

Third-Party Presidential Candidates		
Below are some third-party or independent candidates in the twentieth century who received a significant percentage of the vote.		
Candidate	Party	% of vote
Theodore Roosevelt (1912)	Progressive Party	27
Eugene Debs (1912)	Socialist Party	7
Robert M. LaFoliete (1924)	Progressive Party	17
George Wallace (1968)	American Independent Party	14
John B. Anderson (1980)	National Unity Campaign	7
H. Ross Perot (1992)	(Independent)	19
H. Ross Perot (1996)	Reform Party	9
Ralph Nader (2000)	Green Party	3

3. **Based on what you have learned about third parties in American politics, what can you conclude about the elections listed in the chart above?**

   A Neither the Democratic nor the Republican Party held a nominating convention in these election years.

   B Neither the Democratic nor the Republican nominee was able to win enough electoral votes to become president.

   C Neither the Democratic nor the Republican candidate addressed a set of issues that was important to some voters.

   D Neither the Democratic nor the Republican candidate was able to get enough support to form a coalition government.

4. **Before the election of 1912, Roosevelt broke away from the Republican Party. Although he and the Republican Party candidate drew more votes together than the Democratic candidate, the Democrat won the presidency. Based on this, what can you conclude?**

   F In the past, third-party candidates were very powerful.

   G Third parties can influence the outcome of an election.

   H Third parties always benefit Democrats over Republicans.

   J People are usually more loyal to a person than they are to a political party.

5. **Although third-party candidates have won a high percentage of votes, the chart shows that none has won the presidency in the 20ᵗʰ century. What is the most likely explanation for this?**

   A Third-party candidates have less money than candidates representing the two major parties.

   B Third-party members donate more money to political campaigns than members of the major parties.

   C Third-party candidates are less experienced at campaigning than the Democratic and Republican parties.

   D Third party candidates usually focus on issues that usually get absorbed into the Democratic or Republican tickets.

Political Campaigns and Elections

Political campaigns give voters information about candidates and issues, but the responsibility for investigating, understanding, and making informed decisions resides with each voter.

Directions: Read the following questions and choose the best answer.

6. Look at the political cartoon.

What does the image of President Theodore Roosevelt pushing the elephant up the hill most likely symbolize?

F It symbolizes the push to protect the habitats of the African elephant.

G It symbolizes the struggle that presidents must endure while in office.

H It symbolizes Roosevelt's resolve to get Republicans to back the Panama Canal.

J It symbolizes the dilemma of using one elephant to help build the Panama Canal.

Directions: Look at the chart. Then answer questions 7 and 8.

2000 Presidential Election				
Party	Candidate	Electoral Votes	Popular Votes	% of Popular Vote
Republican	George W. Bush	271	50,455,156	47.9
Democrat	Albert Gore, Jr.	266	50,992,335	48.4
Green	Ralph Nader	0	2,882,738	2.7

7. In presidential elections, how does the popular vote differ from the electoral vote?

A The popular vote is made by the legislatures of each state, whereas the electoral vote is determined by each state's electors.

B The electoral vote is determined by electors of each state, whereas the popular vote is the total number of votes cast by citizens.

C The popular vote, which is the number of votes cast by citizens, determines the outcome of elections, whereas the electoral vote is symbolic.

D The electoral vote is cast by senators and representatives in each state, whereas the popular vote is the total number of votes cast by qualified voters.

8. **What can you conclude based on the information in this chart?**
   - **F** Ralph Nader was a relatively unknown candidate at the time of the election.
   - **G** Without a third-party candidate, George W. Bush would have won the popular vote.
   - **H** It is possible for a candidate to win the presidency without winning the popular vote.
   - **J** Of all the candidates, George W. Bush ran the most effective and efficient campaign.

The Influence of Interest Groups

Interest groups influence the political process through public advocacy, by campaigning during elections, and by donating money to candidates.

Directions: Read the excerpt. Then answer questions 9 and 10.

. . . we are expected to govern with integrity, good will, clear convictions, and a servant's heart. I pledge to all Americans that I will carry myself in this spirit as vice president of the United States. This was the spirit that brought me to the governor's office, when I took on the old politics as usual in Juneau . . . when I stood up to the special interests, the lobbyists, big oil companies, and the good-ol' boys network.

—Governor Sarah Palin, 2008 Republican National Convention Address

9. **Which definition fits the meaning of the term *lobbyists*?**
   - **A** an organized group who share common values and goals
   - **B** people whose job is to influence public officials toward a particular opinion
   - **C** people who work together to raise money for a particular political candidate
   - **D** a group with common concerns who work together to sway government policy

10. **Why do you think Governor Palin made a point of mentioning her opposition to lobbyists?**
    - **F** Lobbyists nominate and campaign for candidates for elected office.
    - **G** Lobbyists represent only Democratic candidates or liberal interest groups.
    - **H** Lobbyists often testify at government hearings for or against proposed laws.
    - **J** Lobbyists charge high fees for their services and often represent wealthy interests.

Test-Taking Tip

Use your prior knowledge when making inferences about a passage on a test. Before reading the passage, read the title, look at any illustrations or graphics that accompany it, and skim the text for any words that are highlighted or repeated throughout. Based on these, use what you already know about words and ideas mentioned to predict what topics you expect to be discussed in the passage. While you read, combine details in the text with what you already know to make inferences and to better understand what you are reading.

This lesson will help you define and identify examples of public policy and describe how public policies are made. Use it with Core Lesson 2.3 *Contemporary Public Policy* to reinforce and apply your knowledge.

Key Concept

Actions taken by the government to address concerns of the voting public are known as public policies.

Core Skills & Practices

- Evaluate Reasoning
- Draw Conclusions

What Is Contemporary Public Policy?

One of the key jobs of the government is to create policies that address and solve problems that affect its citizens.

Directions: Read the excerpt. Then answer the questions that follow.

The preamble to the Constitution identifies a set of national policy goals that contemporary administrations continue to strive for.

We the People of the United States, in Order to form a more perfect Union, establish Justice, insure domestic Tranquility, provide for the common defence, promote the general Welfare, and secure the Blessings of Liberty to ourselves and our Posterity, do ordain and establish this Constitution for the United States of America.

1. **What is the best definition of the word *domestic* as it is used in this passage?**
   A comfortable
   B household
   C internal
   D supportive

2. **What is the best definition of the word *posterity* as used in this passage?**
   F other countries
   G to be prosperous
   H future generations
   J states within the Union

Test-Taking Tip

Remember that when answering vocabulary questions, the correct answer is not always the primary dictionary definition. Combine the context clues given to you in the passage with what you know about the author's purpose to help you determine the intended meaning of the word.

Directions: Read the following questions and choose the best answer.

3. **Which level of government would determine the public policy outlining registration for selective service?**

   A city

   B country

   C federal

   D state

4. **Although state and local governments write public policies, the federal government must write federal public policies to**

   F exert control over state and local governments

   G follow the guidelines set out in the Constitution

   H establish laws that everyone in the nation must follow

   J create examples for state and local governments to follow

5. **Which policy would fall under the responsibility of city government?**

   A defining military eligibility requirements

   B setting sanitation and waste collection standards

   C establishing trade practices with foreign countries

   D defining requirements for obtaining a driver's license

6. **Which public policy would <u>best</u> be described as a public safety policy?**

   F Seatbelts must be worn by all passengers in a moving vehicle.

   G Trucks cannot exceed posted weight limits on public highways.

   H All vehicles must pass an emissions test before being issued a license plate.

   J Drivers must carry medical liability coverage through their auto insurance carrier.

7. **Who is responsible for implementing public policy?**

   A Congress

   B Supreme Court

   C government agencies

   D special interest groups

8. **Rules of guidelines that apply to a specific institution would <u>best</u> be classified as which of the following?**

   F public policy

   G policy formation

   H policy evaluation

   J policy implementation

How National Policy Is Made

Establishing national policy is a complex process that begins with identifying a problem.

Directions: Look at the chart. Then answer questions 9–11.

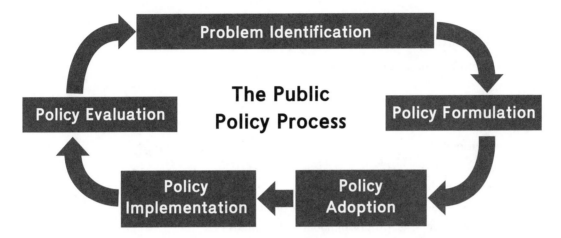

9. **What does the shape of this flow chart tell you about the policy-making process?**

    A By law, government policies can only last one year and have to be renewed.

    B Any policy solution to one problem will always cause another problem.

    C Policy-based solutions to problems are never really successful.

    D Shaping and refining public policy is an ongoing process.

10. **Suppose the Department of Health and Human Services implemented a policy of providing free flu shots to citizens. Which of these steps would most likely follow this step in the public policy process?**

    F Health care advocates would work with lawmakers to shape the policy.

    G Congress would pass a law authorizing the distribution of free flu shots.

    H Public advocacy groups would identify a sharp rise in the number of flu fatalities.

    J Medical researchers would examine the benefits of or problems with the program.

11. **Which step in this process would most likely involve the participation of an interest group?**

    A policy adoption

    B policy formation

    C policy evaluation

    D policy implementation

Influences on Public Policy

The government makes public policy, but it is the relationship between the citizens and their government, mostly through the voting process, that influences which policies are made. Special interest groups and lobbyists also influence public policy through public advocacy or financial support.

Directions: Read the questions and choose the best answer.

12. **Which issue would most likely be taken up by a special interest group?**

   F Campaign finance reform

   G Increasing voter registration

   H Preventing texting while driving

   J Relaxing health care regulations

13. **How do lobbyists differ from special interest groups?**

   A Lobbyists represent special interest groups before members of Congress.

   B Lobbyists try to influence special interest groups in public policy matters.

   C Special interest groups promote specific issues; lobbyists promote a range of issues.

   D Special interest groups try to influence public opinion; lobbyists try to influence Congress.

Directions: Read the excerpt. Then answer questions 14 through 16.

It is said that lobbying itself is an evil and a danger. We agree that lobbying by personal contact may be an evil and a potential danger to the best in legislative processes. It is said that indirect lobbying by the pressure of public opinion on the Congress is an evil and a danger. That is not an evil; it is a good, the healthy essence of the democratic process.

—US Court of Appeals Ruling in *Rumely* v. *United States,* 1952

14. **Which activity best describes the process of lobbying mentioned in this passage?**

   F raising awareness about key issues to help voters

   G persuading public officials to adopt particular positions

   H monitoring public officials to make sure they are not taking bribes

   J electing officials who support policies that help the general public

15. **According to this ruling, which type of lobbying practice might be considered "a potential danger to the best in legislative processes"?**

   A giving testimony before Congress

   B preparing informational reports for lawmakers

   C hiring a public relations firm to promote an issue

   D personally buying lunch or dinner for government officials

16. **This passage shows that citizens can indirectly influence public policy by**

   F sending a lobbyist to Congress

   G evaluating the effectiveness of policies

   H demanding change from elected officials

   J buying an expensive gift for an elected official

This lesson will help you understand the causes of the American Revolution, identify documents that shaped US democratic traditions, summarize provisions of the Articles of Confederation, and understand how and why the Constitution was developed. Use it with Core Lesson 3.1 *American Revolution* to reinforce and apply your knowledge.

Key Concept

After defeating the British, the new United States established a democratic government built on a foundation of English laws and government.

Core Skills & Practices

- Summarize Ideas
- Analyze Cause and Effect

English Colonies in America

British colonies were established in North American beginning in the late sixteenth century by people seeking religious freedom, economic gain, and a new life.

Directions: Read the excerpt. Then answer questions 1 through 4.

Having undertaken . . . a voyage to plant the first colony in [North America], do . . . covenant and combine ourselves together into a civil body politic, for our better ordering and preservation . . . and by virtue hereof to enact, constitute and frame such just and equal laws, ordinances, acts, constitutions and offices, from time to time as shall be thought most meet and convenient for the general good of the Colony . . .

—The Mayflower Compact

1. **What was the purpose of this document?**

   A to give the Pilgrims large portions of land in Massachusetts

   B to explain why the Pilgrims broke with the Church of England

   C to authorize Sir Walter Raleigh to set up a colony in North America

   D to establish the rules by which the Pilgrims would govern themselves

2. **How were the settlers who created this document different from the people who settled in Pennsylvania?**

   F Pennsylvania did not have a written law code.

   G The people who settled in Pennsylvania were not from England.

   H Settlers in Pennsylvania were more tolerant of religious differences.

   J The Pennsylvania colony was not as successful as the Massachusetts colony.

3. **This document is an early example of a**

   A bill of rights

   B constitution

   C charter

   D law

4. **What is the definition of the word *colony* as it is used in the excerpt?**

   F a market for another country's goods

   G a land controlled by another nation

   H a religious organization

   J a voyage of discovery

The American Revolution

Taxes and other policies set forth by the British King and Parliament were deemed unfair by many colonists.

Directions: Read the excerpt below. Then answer questions 5 through 7.

Let these *truths* be indelibly impressed on our minds—*that* we *cannot be* HAPPY, *without being* FREE—that we cannot be free, *without being secure in our property*—that *we* cannot be secure in our property, *if, without our consent, others may, as by right, take it away*—that *taxes imposed on us by parliament,* do thus take it away—that *duties laid for the sole purpose of raising money,* are taxes—that *attempts* to lay such duties *should be instantly and firmly opposed*—that this opposition can never be effectual, *unless it is the united effort . . .*

—excerpt from "Letter XII," *Letters from a Farmer in Pennsylvania*
by John Dickinson, 1768

5. **Dickinson was most likely writing in opposition to what?**

   A the Townshend Acts

   B the Boston Massacre

   C the American Revolution

   D the Continental Congress

6. **Many colonists responded to the taxes mentioned in Dickinson's letter by participating in**

   F the burning of their fields

   G Continental Congress

   H attacks on troops

   J boycotts

7. **What happened as a result of the Boston Tea Party?**

   A Parliament repealed the Stamp Act.

   B Parliament passed new restrictive laws.

   C British troops fired on protesters in Boston.

   D King George III declared war on the colonies.

Directions: Read the excerpt below. Then answer questions 8 through 10.

We therefore beseech your Majesty, that your royal authority and influence may be graciously interposed to procure us relief from our afflicting fears and jealousies . . . and to settle peace through every part of our Dominions . . . and that, in the mean time, measures may be taken for preventing the further destruction of the lives of your Majesty's subjects; and that such statutes as more immediately distress any of your Majesty's Colonies, may be repealed.

8. **This passage was most likely taken from the**
   F   Declaration of Independence
   G   Articles of Confederation
   H   Olive Branch Petition
   J   Mayflower Compact

9. **This document was written as an immediate response to the**
   A   Stamp Act and the Townshend Acts
   B   Battle of Lexington and Concord
   C   Boston Massacre
   D   Tea Party

10. **How did the King of England respond to this document?**
   F   He rejected it.
   G   He tried to negotiate.
   H   He acknowledged the complaints.
   J   He made a proposal to Parliament.

Directions: Read the excerpt. Then answer questions 11 and 12.

The war with France greatly increased Britain's territory in North America. It also created problems. The war nearly doubled Britain's national debt. Although nearly broke, Britain had to pay for additional soldiers to defend the new territory. The British government insisted that the colonists should help keep the peace and pay part of the cost of defense. The colonists were forced to pay the salaries of soldiers, feed them, and provide them with housing. In 1764, the British Parliament placed import duties, or fees, on sugar and other products shipped into the colonies. In 1765, it taxed legal documents and other printed matter.

11. **Which sentence states the central idea of this passage?**
   A   The British government insisted that the colonists should help keep the peace and pay part of the cost of defense.
   B   The colonists were forced to pay the salaries of soldiers, feed them, and provide them with housing.
   C   In 1765, it taxed legal documents and other printed matter.
   D   The war nearly doubled Britain's national debt.

12. What was the cause and effect of British action in the 1760s?

   F Because Britain could not afford the additional soldiers needed to defend the new territory; the British government insisted that the colonists pay part of the cost of defense.

   G Because the colonists were forced to pay for soldiers' food and lodging, the British Parliament placed import duties on products shipped to the colonies.

   H Because the colonists paid for soldiers' food and lodging, the British Parliament began taxing legal documents and other printed materials.

   J Because Britain's territory in North America increased; the British Parliament received more income from duties.

The Confederation Period

With the passage of a document called the Articles of Confederation, these American colonies joined together under flawed, central government but eventually ratified a new Constitution and became the United States of America.

Directions: Read the following questions and choose the best answer.

13. What caused the creation of a new US Constitution in 1788?

   A States could not agree on the Virginia Plan.

   B Anti-Federalists opposed the Articles of Confederation.

   C Congress wanted the power to declare war and borrow money.

   D The Articles of Confederation created a weak federal government.

14. What is one way the Articles of Confederation differed from the new Constitution?

   F Under the Articles, the states held many powers, but under the Constitution, they have few.

   G Under the Articles, Congress had the power to tax, but under the Constitution, Congress lacks this power.

   H Under the Articles, the legislative branch had one house, but under the Constitution, the legislative branch has two houses.

   J Under the Articles, the president holds the power to declare war, but under the Constitution, the Congress holds this power.

15. On what central idea did the Great Compromise differ from the Virginia Plan?

   A The federal government would consist of three branches.

   B The legislature was given the power to coin and borrow money.

   C Congress would now have the power to declare war and make peace.

   D State population would determine representation in the House of Representatives.

✅ Test-Taking Tip

When answering multiple-choice questions, use the process of elimination. That is, first eliminate all answers you know are definitely incorrect. Then analyze the remaining options to determine which one is the correct answer.

This lesson will help you understand how the United States grew geographically, identify the causes and consequences of the War of 1812, and explain how westward expansion affected Native Americans. Use it with Core Lesson 3.2 *A New Nation* to reinforce and apply your knowledge.

Key Concept

After the Revolutionary War, the United States endured conflicts within and struggled with other countries as well.

Core Skills & Practices

- Sequence Events
- Relate Ideas within Text

The Growth of the Nation

The expansion of the new United States was aided by the Northwest Ordinance of 1787 and the newly ratified Constitution, which created a federal government with a much stronger executive branch than that of the Articles of Confederation.

Directions: Read the following questions and choose the best answer.

1. **Read the information in the box.**

   So soon as there shall be five thousand free male inhabitants of full age in the district, upon giving proof thereof to the governor, they shall receive authority, with time and place, to elect a representative from their counties or townships to represent them in the general assembly . . .

   This passage is most likely taken from the

   A Treaty of Paris

   B Articles of Confederation

   C United States Constitution

   D Northwest Ordinance of 1787

2. **Which definition fits the meaning of the term *territory*?**

   F an area of land controlled by a government

   G an area of land whose borders are unclear

   H a gift of land from one nation to another

   J land that is settled by a group of people

Test-Taking Tip

Some test items ask about specific words or phrases, paragraphs, or sections of a passage. Before answering a question about a text detail, reread the related sentence or paragraph whether or not the item directs you to reread it. As you reread, focus on what the question is about. For example, if the item is about the meaning of a word, think about how the word is used as you reread.

3. **How did the Land Ordinance of 1785 initiate a sequence of events that led to the admission of five states to the Union?**

   A It allowed settlers to create governments.

   B It prohibited the taxation of land in the Northwest Territory.

   C It made land available for a low price, attracting many settlers.

   D It set up law enforcement agencies, easing fears of landowners.

4. **Read the chart describing the roles and responsibilities of executive offices.**

   ### Roles and Responsibilities of the Executive Departments

Department	Leader's Title	Main Area of Responsibility
State Department	Secretary of State	dealing with other nations
Treasury Department	Secretary of the Treasury	looking after the nation's finances
War Department	Secretary of War	defending the nation

   The offices described in this chart were created by

   F popular vote

   G an act of Congress

   H presidential appointment

   J an article of the Constitution

5. **What led to the Treaty of Greenville in 1795?**

   A British troops would not withdraw from American forts.

   B The Shawnee and other tribes attacked white settlers in the Ohio Valley.

   C The French agreed to sell lands west of the Mississippi to the United States.

   D Spain was worried about American interference in its territories in North America.

Directions: Read the excerpt. Then answer questions 6 and 7.

Louisiana Purchase Treaty (1803)

Robert Livingston and James Monroe closed on the sweetest real estate deal of the millennium when they signed the Louisiana Purchase Treaty in Paris on April 30, 1803. They were authorized to pay France up to $10 million for the port of New Orleans and the Floridas. When offered the entire territory of Louisiana—an area larger than Great Britain, France, Germany, Italy, Spain and Portugal combined—the American negotiators swiftly agreed to a price of $15 million.

Although President Thomas Jefferson was a strict interpreter of the Constitution who wondered if the U.S. Government was authorized to acquire new territory, he was also a visionary who dreamed of an "empire for liberty" that would stretch across the entire continent. As Napoleon threatened to take back the offer, Jefferson squelched whatever doubts he had and prepared to occupy a land of unimaginable riches.

6. **Why would a strict interpretation of the Constitution have prevented Thomas Jefferson from moving forward with the Louisiana Purchase?**

   F It would have kept him from acquiring the land because there was no specific provision for this action in the Constitution.

   G It would have required him to get approval from each of the states before proceeding with this acquisition.

   H It would have kept him from asking Congress to raise taxes to pay for the land.

   J It would have kept him from entering into a treaty with a foreign country.

7. **What did Jefferson consider more important than constitutionality in making this decision?**

   A eradicating slavery in the new territory

   B his popularity with the American people

   C providing for future growth of the nation

   D removing all foreign landowners from America

The War of 1812

Issues with Great Britain continued for several years after the American Revolution ended, and soon, war again became inevitable.

Directions: Read the following questions and choose the best answer.

8. **Which best supports the idea that the Battle of New Orleans was unnecessary?**

   F The war had ended with the Treaty of Ghent.

   G The British attacked and burned Washington, D.C.

   H The British had surrendered when they failed to take Baltimore.

   J Britain agreed to give the United States its North American territory.

9. **Why did Western and Southern voters tend to be more supportive of the War of 1812 than their Northern counterparts?**

   A Southern and Western voters elected to Congress Revolutionary War heroes who promoted another war with Britain.

   B Britain seized ships filled with Southern goods and inflamed tensions between Western settlers and Indians.

   C Britain cut off trade with Southern and Western states but continued trading with Northern states.

   D More Northern voters were of British descent, whereas Southern and Western voters were not.

10. **Which of these was an outcome of the War of 1812?**

   F the signing of Jay's Treaty

   G increased tensions with Spain

   H an upsurge in American nationalism

   J the establishment of a new American navy

Manifest Destiny

In the early 1800s, Americans were angry with the British for impressing American sailors and for taking American ships. On June 18, 1812, Congress declared war against Britain. In 1815, the Treaty of Ghent ended the war. Britain and the United States agreed to restore any territories taken during the war.

Directions: Read the excerpt. Then answer questions 11 through 13.

The whole continent of North America appears to be destined by Divine Providence to be peopled by one *nation*, speaking one language, professing one general system of religious and political principles, and accustomed to one general tenor of social usages and customs. For the common happiness of them all, for their peace and prosperity, I believe it is indispensable that they should be associated in one federal Union.

—John Quincy Adams

11. Which event can be seen as a direct result of the beliefs espoused by Adams?

A the Battle of Tippecanoe

B the annexation of Texas

C the War of 1812

D Jay's Treaty

12. In this quote, John Quincy Adams is expressing an idea that became known as

F the Union Proclamation

G Westward Expansion

H the Land Ordinance

J Manifest Destiny

13. Which was one of the negative consequences of Adams' declaration?

A war with Spain

B the Louisiana Purchase

C Native American removal

D the Battle of New Orleans

This lesson will help you understand the causes and effects of the Civil War and analyze a writer's point of view and use of persuasive language. Use it with Core Lesson 3.3 *Civil War and Reconstruction* to reinforce and apply your knowledge.

Key Concept

The Civil War began as an attempt to preserve the Union, but it ended with the abolition of slavery in the United States.

Core Skills & Practices

- Recognize Persuasive Language
- Analyze Point of View

Slavery in the United States

As slavery grew to become an essential part of the South's economy, many northerners—appalled by its human cost—began the movement to end slavery.

Directions: Read the following questions and choose the best answer.

1. **Enslaved Africans were brought to the American colonies via a route that became known as**

   A the African Trade Route

   B the Missouri Compromise

   C the Underground Railroad

   D the Triangular Trade Route

2. **Which group would most likely have supported the expansion of slavery?**

   F poor farmers

   G factory owners

   H wealthy planters

   J newspaper publishers

3. **Abolitionists were people who**

   A hired farm laborers

   B sold enslaved Africans

   C were opposed to slavery

   D were against the Civil War

4. **What good was transported from the colonies to Africa for trade?**

   A rum

   B sugar

   C molasses

   D enslaved people

Directions: Look at the map. Then answer questions 5 through 7.

5. **Which best explains why it was so important to opponents of slavery that Missouri not enter the Union as a slave state?**

   A Missouri had a higher population of enslaved workers than any other territory.

   B Most of the country's enslaved workers were purchased in markets in Missouri.

   C Its entry would upset the balance between the slave and free states in the Senate.

   D They did not believe that Missouri should have the same rights as the original states.

6. **What other state was created as a result of Missouri's admission to the Union?**

   F Louisiana

   G Maine

   H Michigan

   J Oregon

7. **Which area became closed to slavery by the Missouri Compromise?**

   A New Spain

   B Oregon Territory

   C Michigan Territory

   D Unorganized Territory

Civil War

In 1861, sectional conflict erupted into a full-scale Civil War, as eleven states seceded from the Union.

Directions: Read the excerpt. Then answer questions 8 and 9.

In *your* hands, my dissatisfied fellow-countrymen, and not in *mine*, is the momentous issue of civil war. The Government will not assail *you*. You can have no conflict without being yourselves the aggressors. *You* have no oath registered in heaven to destroy the Government, while I shall have the most solemn one to "preserve, protect, and defend it."

I am loath to close. We are not enemies, but friends. We must not be enemies. Though passion may have strained it must not break our bonds of affection. The mystic chords of memory, stretching from every battlefield and patriot grave to every living heart and hearthstone all over this broad land, will yet swell the chorus of the Union, when again touched, as surely they will be, by the better angels of our nature.

—Abraham Lincoln, First Inaugural Address

8. **Which best explains why Lincoln stressed that the Union would not provoke a civil war?**
    F   Lincoln was not confident in the North's military leadership.
    G   Lincoln still thought the Missouri Compromise would settle the issue.
    H   Lincoln knew that the northern economy depended on southern cotton.
    J   Lincoln did not want to alienate slave states that had stayed in the Union.

9. **Lincoln's speech is characterized by his use of**
    A   patriotic appeals
    B   economic appeals
    C   descriptive language
    D   persuasive language

Directions: Read the following questions and choose the best answer.

10. **Which event signaled the official beginning of the Civil War?**
    F   Battle of Bull Run
    G   attack on Fort Sumter
    H   election of Abraham Lincoln
    J   admission of Missouri as a slave state

11. **What was one major advantage that the South had during the Civil War?**
    A   familiarity with battlegrounds
    B   more factories and materials
    C   more men of military age
    D   naval superiority

Reconstruction

The period after the Civil War is known as Reconstruction, because it was necessary to rebuild the Union and the various forms of destruction caused by the war itself.

Directions: Read the following questions and choose the best answer.

12. **Which sentence best explains why President Johnson required ex-Confederates to swear loyalty to the Union before they could be pardoned?**

    F After the Civil War, every citizen was required to take a loyalty oath.

    G Johnson was planning to rebuild the United States military with Civil War veterans.

    H Johnson did not want the ex-Confederates to take up arms against the Union again.

    J The loyalty oaths helped ensure Johnson's personal safety after Lincoln's assassination.

13. **Northerners eventually turned away from Reconstruction for reasons that could best be classified as**

    A economic

    B ethical

    C political

    D religious

Directions: Read the excerpt. Then answer questions 14 and 15.

Section 1. Neither slavery nor involuntary servitude, except as a punishment for crime whereof the party shall have been duly convicted, shall exist within the United States, or any place subject to their jurisdiction.

14. **Many Southern states responded to this amendment by passing**

    F new amendments

    G property statutes

    H loyalty oaths

    J black codes

15. **This excerpt is most likely taken from the**

    A Thirteenth Amendment

    B Fourteenth Amendment

    C Fifteenth Amendment

    D Sixteenth Amendment

 Test-Taking Tip

When reading a multiple-choice question, read the question first and answer it in your head before reading the answers. That way you won't be overly influenced by possible wrong answers.

This lesson will help you understand why immigrants came to America, identify where they settled, and understand how they were received. Use it with Core Lesson 3.4 *European Settlement and Population of the Americas* to reinforce and apply your knowledge.

Key Concept

As immigrants came to America, they settled in cities and spread throughout the growing West.

Core Skills & Practices

- Summarize Ideas
- Find Details

The Growth of Immigration

The United States not only grew geographically in the period from 1820 to 1920, but it also grew in population due to the more than 33 million immigrants who moved to the United States from other countries.

Directions: Study the map. Then answer questions 1 through 4.

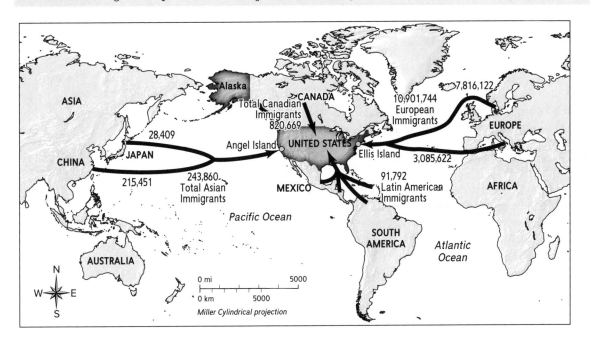

1. **Based on the numbers of immigrants as shown on this map, what region was the source of the largest numbers of immigrants to the United States during this period?**

   A Asia

   B Canada

   C Northern Europe

   D Southern Europe

2. Based on the information in this map, you can conclude that the problem of overcrowding was <u>most</u> pronounced in the

  F midwest

  G northeast

  H south

  J west

3. Based on where they entered the United States as shown on this map, most Latin American immigrants <u>most likely</u> worked as

  A railroad construction workers in the west

  B factory workers in Detroit or Chicago

  C carpenters in the northeast

  D farmers in the southwest

4. Which was a pull factor that led to the increase in immigration illustrated on the map?

  F democracy

  G political oppression

  H poverty

  J religious intolerance

Life in America

By the end of the 19th century, more than half of all Americans were living in cities instead of on farms, encouraging a rise of poor living conditions and three distinct social classes.

Directions: Read the excerpt. Then answer questions 5 through 8.

Be a little careful, please! The hall is dark and you might stumble over the children pitching pennies back there. Not that it would hurt them; kicks and cuffs are their daily diet. They have little else. Here where the hall turns and dives into utter darkness is a step, and another, another. A flight of stairs. You can feel your way, if you cannot see it. Close? Yes! . . . That was a woman filling her pail by the hydrant you just bumped against. The sinks are in the hallway, that all the tenants may have access—and all be poisoned alike by their summer stenches. Hear the pump squeak! . . . In summer, when a thousand thirsty throats pant for a cooling drink in this block, it is worked in vain. But the saloon, whose open door you passed in the hall, is always there. The smell of it has followed you up. Here is a door. Listen! That short hacking cough, that tiny, helpless wail—what do they mean?

—excerpt from *How the Other Half Lives* by Jacob Riis, 1890

5. The author of this passage is <u>most likely</u> describing life in a

  A city center

  B farm

  C suburb

  D tenement house

6. **This passage shows that one of the greatest dangers facing immigrants was**

   F gang violence

   G poor sanitation

   H political corruption

   J unsafe working conditions

7. **The "other half" to whom Riis is referring in the title of this excerpt is <u>most likely</u> the**

   A unemployed

   B middle class

   C poor working class

   D wealthy upper class

8. **What would have been the <u>most likely</u> pull factor to draw people to live in such difficult conditions as those described in the passage?**

   F falling farm prices

   G the opportunity to find work in the city

   H the opportunity to live near the city center

   J technology in farming reduced the need for farmworkers

Discrimination Against Immigrants

Adapting to life in America was not easy for many immigrants, and their differences often made them targets of discrimination.

Directions: Study the chart. Then answer questions 9 through 12.

Immigration to the United States, 1870–1920

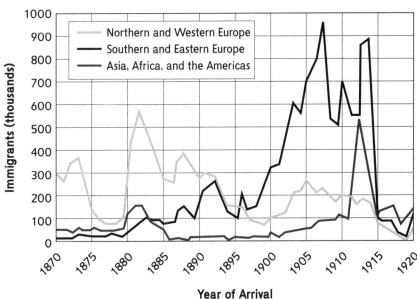

9. **Which group was <u>most</u> opposed to the increase in immigration illustrated on the chart?**

   A Catholics

   B nativists

   C Progressives

   D women

10. **Which sentence <u>best</u> explains why some Americans opposed this new wave of immigration?**

    F Immigrants tended to push native-born citizens out of the city centers.

    G Immigrants from Asia and Eastern Europe were opposed to democratic institutions.

    H Immigrants from southern and eastern Europe had different religions and traditions.

    J Immigrants built new factories that caused pollution and unsafe working conditions.

11. **Which one of these options <u>best</u> explains the decline in Asian, African, and Latin American immigration between 1880 and 1885?**

    A the Mexican Revolution

    B the Chinese Exclusion Act

    C the Progressive Movement

    D the Spanish-American War

12. **During which five-year period did the steepest drop in immigration from Southern and Eastern Europe occur?**

    F 1880–1885

    G 1890–1895

    H 1910–1915

    J 1915–1920

 Test-Taking Tip

Before answering questions related to a graph, be sure to identify what is represented on each axis. Then carefully check how the values on each axis increase or decrease.

This lesson will help you identify the causes of World War I and its effects on Europe and the United States, and it will explain how and why the League of Nations was formed. Use it with Core Lesson 4.1 *World War I* to reinforce and apply your knowledge.

Key Concept	**Core Skills & Practices**
World War I resulted from alliances being formed throughout the world.	• Make Predictions • Sequence Events

The United States Becomes a World Power

By the 1890s, nationalism and imperialism were two sides of the coin that made the United States a nation to be respected before the advent of World War I.

Directions: Read the excerpt. Then answer questions 1 through 3.

The Spanish-American War grew out of the American public's growing desire to expand American territory and interests and out of a general "war fever."

Several of the larger American newspapers began to capitalize on the Cuban struggle for independence from Spain, sensationalizing abuses Spanish military forces were committing against the Cubans.

Public outrage reached its peak with the sinking of the battleship [USS] *Maine*, which was sent to the Havana harbor to protect U.S. citizens and property in Cuba. Though the cause of the explosion was never discovered, President McKinley approved a congressional resolution demanding immediate Spanish withdrawal from Cuba. A few days later, Spain declared war.

The congressional resolution stated that the United States was not acting to secure an empire. However, the terms of the Treaty of Paris that officially ended the war required that Spain cede the Philippines, Puerto Rico, and Guam to the United States. For good or ill, the United States had expanded.

1. **According to this writer, American involvement in Cuba was <u>most directly</u> triggered by**

   A a belief that democracy is the only fair form of government

   B an overriding desire to maintain peace in the Western Hemisphere

   C a sense of outrage about danger to American lives and property abroad

   D a desire to help and protect the less economically fortunate in this world

2. **According to this excerpt, in its resolution demanding Spanish withdrawal from Cuba, the United States Congress wanted to avoid appearing as though it was following a policy of**

   F imperialism

   G industrialization

   H militarism

   J nationalism

3. **To protect the United States's new position in the world, Congress allocated money for building**

   A markets for American goods

   B the supply of steel and oil

   C more miles of railroad

   D a larger navy

World War I

The Great War, later known as World War I, began in Europe in 1914. Aa series of alliances brought more and more countries, including the United States, into the conflict.

Directions: Read the following questions and choose the best answer.

4. **Why did Austria-Hungary's declaration of war against Serbia lead to a wider conflict?**

   F Serbia had a large colonial empire.

   G Serbia was allied with the Allied Powers.

   H Franz Ferdinand was beloved throughout Europe.

   J Austria-Hungary's actions angered the United States.

5. **Austria-Hungary was involved in a wider alliance with**

   A Germany and the Ottoman Empire

   B Great Britain and France

   C Serbia and Russia

   D the United States

Directions: Read the excerpt below. Then answer questions 6 through 8.

We intend to begin on the first of February unrestricted submarine warfare. We shall endeavor in spite of this to keep the United States of America neutral. In the event of this not succeeding, we make Mexico a proposal of alliance on the following basis: make war together, make peace together, generous financial support and an understanding on our part that Mexico is to reconquer the lost territory in Texas, New Mexico, and Arizona.

6. **This passage was most likely written by a foreign minister from which country?**

   F Germany

   G Great Britain

   H Russia

   J Serbia

7. **Which sentence best explains the reason for the United States' neutrality before this document was made public?**

   A Some Americans favored the Allies, but others favored the Central Powers.

   B Germany had formed an alliance with Mexico, an ally of the United States.

   C The United States wanted peace but favored Serbian independence.

   D The United States was not certain which side would win the war.

8. The "unrestricted submarine warfare" described in the excerpt caused

   F Russia's withdrawal from the war

   G the creation of the Fourteen Points

   H the destruction of Great Britain's navy

   J Congress' declaration of war on Germany

Directions: Study the map. Then answer the question that follows.

9. What was one of the biggest disadvantages faced by Germany at the beginning of the war?

   A It was separated from its allies.

   B It had to fight a war on two fronts.

   C It was surrounded by neutral nations.

   D It had no access to the Mediterranean Sea.

After the War

When the war was over, the victorious countries wanted to create a setting in Europe that would ensure peace. President Wilson's plans for world peace were accepted in Europe, but not in the United States.

Directions: Read the excerpt. Then answer questions 10 and 11.

We entered this war because violations of right had occurred which touched us to the quick and made the life of our own people impossible unless they were corrected and the world secure once for all against their recurrence. What we demand in this war, therefore, is nothing peculiar to ourselves. It is that the world be made fit and safe to live in; and particularly that it be made safe for every peace-loving nation which, like our own, wishes to live its own life, determine its own institutions, be assured of justice and fair dealing by the other peoples of the world as against force and selfish aggression. All the peoples of the world are in effect partners in this interest, and for our own part we see very clearly that unless justice be done to others it will not be done to us.

—President Woodrow Wilson, January 8, 1918

10. What was President Wilson was <u>most likely</u> expressing his support for in the excerpt above?

   F the Big Four

   G the Central Powers

   H the League of Nations

   J the Paris Peace Conference

11. This excerpt also reflects Wilson's support for the Treaty of Versailles. How did the views of the United States Senate differ from those of Wilson?

   A Most senators were opposed to the US involvement in the war.

   B Most senators felt that the treaty did not do enough to punish Germany.

   C Most senators refused to recognize the new countries created by the treaty.

   D Most senators were opposed to the League of Nations created by the treaty.

Directions: Study the map. Then answer the question that follows.

Europe After World War I

New nations

12. Which region of Europe was <u>most</u> affected by the creation of new countries under the Treaty of Versailles?

   F Eastern Europe

   G Northern Europe

   H Southern Europe

   J Western Europe

 Test-Taking Tip

When you are answering questions involving a map, be sure to read the question first so you can know what to look for when you study the map.

This lesson will help you understand the events that led to World War II, the alliances formed during the war, why the United States entered the war, and how life in the United States was affected by the war. Use it with Core Lesson 4.2 *World War II* to reinforce and apply your knowledge.

Key Concept

After World War I, three totalitarian governments formed in Europe and began World War II.

Core Skills & Practices

- Identify Author's Bias
- Understand the Main Idea

The Rise of Dictators

In the years following World War I, totalitarian leaders such as Adolf Hitler and Benito Mussolini were able to seize power by taking advantage of Europe's political and economic instability.

Directions: Read the excerpt. Then answer questions 1 through 4.

Excerpt from Adolf Hitler—Speech before the Reichstag January 30, 1937

Four years ago, when I was entrusted with the Chancellorship and therewith the leadership of the nation, I took upon myself the bitter duty of restoring the honor of a nation . . . forced to live as a pariah . . . The internal order which we created among the German people offered the conditions necessary to reorganize the army and also made it possible for me to throw off those shackles which we felt to be the deepest disgrace ever branded on a people. . . .

I now state here that, in accordance with the restoration of equality of rights, I shall divest the German Railways and the Reichsbank of the forms under which they have hitherto functioned and shall place them absolutely under the sovereign control of the Government of the German Reich.

1. **How was Hitler able to assume control of Germany's railroads and banks?**
   - **A** The Treaty of Versailles authorized Hitler to take control of these industries.
   - **B** Hitler had suspended the constitution and could pass whatever laws he wanted.
   - **C** German citizens had voted to turn the railroads and banks over to the government.
   - **D** The German Reichstag budgeted the money necessary to buy the railroads and banks.

2. **The term that is used to describe a government that controls the politics, economy, and culture of a nation is**
   - **F** nationalist
   - **G** republican
   - **H** socialist
   - **J** totalitarian

✔ Test-Taking Tip

When you are answering passage-based questions, it is sometimes a good idea to skim the passage first to get an idea of the author's general purpose and tone. Then skim the questions so you are aware of what to look for as you read the passage.

3. **Which phrase from the passage is an example of bias in Hitler's speech?**
   A   those shackles which we felt to be the deepest disgrace ever branded on a people
   B   place them absolutely under the sovereign control of the Government
   C   the internal order which we created among the German people
   D   four years ago, when I was entrusted with the Chancellorship

4. **The "shackles" Hitler refers to in his speech most likely refer to**
   F   fascist policies
   G   the United Nations
   H   the Great Depression
   J   reparations for World War I

World War II

Provoked by Hitler's conquest of much of Western Europe and by a direct assault by Japanese forces, the United States entered World War II in 1941.

Directions: Read the excerpt. Then answer questions 5 and 6.

Soldiers, Sailors and Airmen of the Allied Expeditionary Force! You are about to embark upon the Great Crusade, toward which we have striven these many months. . . the destruction of the German war machine, the elimination of Nazi tyranny over the oppressed peoples of Europe, and security for ourselves in a free world.

Your task will not be an easy one. Your enemy is well trained, well equipped and battle hardened. . .

Much has happened since the Nazi triumphs of 1940–41. . . . great defeats, in open battle, . . . Our air offensive has seriously reduced their strength in the air and their capacity to wage war on the ground. Our Home Fronts have given us an overwhelming superiority in weapons and munitions of war. . .

The tide has turned! The free men of the world are marching together to Victory!

I have full confidence in your courage. . . We will accept nothing less than full Victory!

Good luck! And let us beseech the blessing of Almighty God upon this great and noble undertaking.

—General Dwight D. Eisenhower, June 2, 1944

5. **Which event is one of the "Nazi triumphs" to which Eisenhower refers in his address?**
   A   the Battle of Stalingrad
   B   the defeat of Mussolini
   C   the attack on Pearl Harbor
   D   the conquest of the Balkans

5. The first paragraph of this excerpt expresses a United States policy toward combating communism that would later be known as

   A aggression

   B containment

   C engagement

   D resistance

6. Which of these demonstrated how President Truman was able to put the second part of Kennan's analysis into action?

   F Marshall Plan

   G Yalta conference

   H Bay of Pigs Invasion

   J Cuban missile crisis

7. Which international organization carried out Kennan's ideas?

   A North Atlantic Treaty Organization

   B United Nations Security Council

   C Yalta Conference

   D Warsaw Pact

8. President Truman responded to the Soviet Union's blockade of West Berlin by

   F invading East Germany

   G airlifting supplies into West Berlin

   H withdrawing from the United Nations

   J building bomb shelters in the United States

Directions: Read the following questions and choose the best answer.

9. President Kennedy responded to the Soviet Union's demand that West Berlin be joined with East Berlin under a Communist government by

   A building the Berlin Wall

   B agreeing to the demands

   C sending troops to West Berlin

   D signing a peace treaty with East Germany

10. The border dividing Europe between western nations and Soviet-influenced nations became known as the

   F Demilitarized Zone

   G Iron Curtain

   H Maginot Line

   J Western Front

11. One feature of the United Nations was the veto power of the five permanent members of the Security Council, including the United States and the Soviet Union. This was a shortcoming because

A both the United States and the Soviet Union wished to use force to settle most disputes.

B the United States and the Soviet Union refused to share power on the Security Council.

C the Soviet Union demanded a leadership position on the Security Council.

D the United States and the Soviet Union disagreed on many important issues.

Communism Outside of Europe

As the inauguration of President John Kennedy signaled a new era in American politics, the United States faced new threats in the form of communist governments in Cuba and in Southeast Asia.

Directions: Read the excerpt. Then answer questions 12 through 14.

To those peoples in the huts and villages across the globe struggling to break the bonds of mass misery, we pledge our best efforts to help them help themselves, for whatever period is required—not because the Communists may be doing it, not because we seek their votes, but because it is right. If a free society cannot help the many who are poor, it cannot save the few who are rich.

To our sister republics south of our border, we offer a special pledge—to convert our good words into good deeds—in a new alliance for progress—to assist free men and free governments in casting off the chains of poverty. But this peaceful revolution of hope cannot become the prey of hostile powers. Let all our neighbors know that we shall join with them to oppose aggression or subversion anywhere in the Americas. And let every other power know that this Hemisphere intends to remain the master of its own house.

—President John F. Kennedy, Inaugural Address

12. One reason Kennedy might have been especially concerned about the plight of "our sister republics south of the border" was that thousands of refugees were fleeing Cuba to the United States to escape

F Soviet nuclear missiles

G extreme poverty and slavery

H the rule of the catholic church

J the communist government of Fidel Castro

13. Kennedy's critics might have argued that he failed to "oppose aggression" in the Americas by refusing to

A send spy planes over Cuba

B provide air cover for the Bay of Pigs invasion

C remove missile sites from the Turkish-Russian border

D allocate money to build bomb shelters in the United States

14. President Johnson carried on the foreign policy outlined in Kennedy's inaugural address by

F opposing colonial rule in Africa

G holding peace talks with Nikita Khrushchev

H increasing the number of troops in Vietnam

J granting independence to India and Pakistan

This lesson will help you understand the achievements and failures of the Johnson and Nixon administrations and their connections to the collapse of communism. Use it with Core Lesson 4.4 *Societal Changes* to reinforce and apply your knowledge.

Key Concept

During the second half of the twentieth century, the United States struggled with scandals at home and communism abroad.

Core Skills & Practices

- Integrate Concepts Presented in Different Ways
- Paraphrase Information

The Great Society

The presidency of Lyndon Johnson was defined by Great Society programs and the Vietnam War.

Directions: Read the excerpt below. Then answer questions 1 and 2.

The Great Society rests on abundance and liberty for all. It demands an end to poverty and racial injustice, to which we are totally committed in our time. But that is just the beginning. The Great Society is a place where every child can find knowledge to enrich his mind and to enlarge his talents. It is a place where leisure is a welcome chance to build and reflect, not a feared cause of boredom and restlessness. It is a place where the city of man serves not only the needs of the body and the demands of commerce but the desire for beauty and the hunger for community. It is a place where man can renew contact with nature. It is a place which honors creation for its own sake and for what it adds to the understanding of the race. It is a place where men are more concerned with the quality of their goals than the quantity of their goods. But most of all, the Great Society is not a safe harbor, a resting place, a final objective, a finished work. It is a challenge constantly renewed, beckoning us toward a destiny where the meaning of our lives matches the marvelous products of our labor.

—President Lyndon B. Johnson, Great Society Speech, 1964

1. **According to the excerpt, which of these is one major focus of the Great Society?**
   A environmental enrichment
   B greater retirement options
   C greater production of goods
   D increased industrial production

2. **If Great Society programs were entirely successful, according to Johnson, what would be one likely result?**
   F All citizens could buy the products they wanted.
   G All adult citizens would have more leisure time.
   H People of all races would be assured equal rights.
   J Laws would prevent any adverse effects on the environment.

Directions: Read the following questions and choose the best answer.

3. **Under the Great Society, a person who wanted to report charges of discrimination in the workplace could appeal to**

   A VISTA

   B the EEOC

   C the Voting Rights Act

   D the Community Action Program

4. **Which Great Society program fought poverty in cities, rural areas, and reservations?**

   F VISTA

   G EEOC

   H Voting Rights Act

   J Community Action Program

The Nixon Administration

President Richard Nixon ended the Vietnam War and introduced policies of New Federalism but was eventually forced to resign as a result of the Watergate scandal.

Directions: Read the excerpt below. Then answer questions 5 and 6.

Since March, when I first learned that the Watergate affair might in fact be far more serious than I had been led to believe, it has claimed far too much of my time and my attention. Whatever may now transpire in the case, whatever the actions of the grand jury, whatever the outcome of any eventual trials, I must now turn my full attention—and I shall do so—once again to the larger duties of this office. I owe it to this great office that I hold, and I owe it to you—to my country. . . Tomorrow, for example, Chancellor Brandt of West Germany will visit the White House for talks that are a vital element of "The Year of Europe," as 1973 has been called. We are already preparing for the next Soviet-American summit meeting later this year.

This is also a year in which we are seeking to negotiate a mutual and balanced reduction of armed forces in Europe, which will reduce our defense budget and allow us to have funds for other purposes at home so desperately needed. It is the year when the United States and Soviet negotiators will seek to work out the second and even more important round of our talks on limiting nuclear arms and of reducing the danger of a nuclear war that would destroy civilization as we know it. It is a year in which we confront the difficult tasks of maintaining peace in Southeast Asia and in the potentially explosive Middle East.

—President Richard M. Nixon, First Watergate Speech, 1973

5. **At the time Nixon gave this speech, which statement appears to be true?**

   A The House Judiciary Committee had voted for Nixon's impeachment.

   B Transcripts of White House tapes had been provided to the Congress.

   C Five men who had broken into Democratic offices had been arrested.

   D Nixon had decided to resign from the presidency.

6. **Of all the issues mentioned in President Nixon's speech, which one contributed <u>most</u> to his resignation?**

   F terrorism in the Middle East

   G conflict in Southeast Asia

   H nuclear arms control

   J the Watergate affair

Directions: Read the following questions and choose the best answer.

7. **Which of these was an achievement of the Nixon Administration?**

   A Civil Rights Act

   B the Great Society

   C Voting Rights Act

   D Paris Peace Accord

8. **According to the speech, Nixon was focused on which of these instead of the Watergate affair?**

   F ending communism in the Soviet Union

   G reducing the worldwide nuclear threat

   H increasing US military presence overseas

   J reducing taxes for working United States families

Communism in China and the Soviet Union

Improvements in relations between the United States and communist countries and societal changes over many decades eventually led to the birth of democracy in Eastern European nations and the dissolution of the Soviet Union.

Directions: Read the following questions and choose the best answer.

9. **The Strategic Arms Limitation Treaty (SALT), signed in 1972, served what purpose?**

   A to reduce the size of United States and Soviet armies stationed in Europe

   B to freeze the production of long-range offensive missiles

   C to remove restrictions on borders in Eastern Europe

   D to eliminate nuclear weapons worldwide

10. **Communism came to an end in the Soviet Union following what development?**

    F the collapse of the Soviet economy

    G the surrender of Soviet troops to NATO forces

    H Democratic reforms begun by Soviet leader Mikhail Gorbachev

    J a negotiated truce between Soviet leaders and democratic activists in the USSR

11. **Relations between China and the Soviet Union during the Cold War were**

    A strained because of their conflict during World War II

    B close because of their mutual suspicion of the United States

    C close because of their shared status as large communist nations

    D strained because of their large shared border and different interpretations of communism

12. **Relations between China and the Soviet Union during the Cold War were**

F strained because of their conflict during World War II

G close because of their mutual suspicion of the United States

H close because of their shared status as large communist nations

J strained because of their large shared border and different interpretations of communism

13. **Which term best describes the Nixon Administration's policies toward China and the Soviet Union after 1971?**

A appeasement

B brinksmanship

C détente

D isolation

14. **Nixon's visit to China started diplomatic communications that had previously been cut off during which decade?**

F 1930s

G 1940s

H 1950s

J 1960s

 Test-Taking Tip

If you can not identify the correct answer in a question, begin with the one or two answer choices that you know. Eliminate the choices that you know are incorrect, and then select the best option from the remaining choices.

This lesson will help you understand how US government policies changed after the terrorist attacks on September 11, 2001. Use it with Core Lesson 4.5 *Foreign Policy in the 21st Century* to reinforce and apply your knowledge.

Key Concept

In the first decade of the twenty-first century, the United States experienced a terrorist attack that reshaped government and policies.

Core Skills & Practices

- Conduct Research Projects
- Evaluate Evidence

Terrorism in the United States

Terrorist attacks on the United States in the 1990s and 2001 were linked to Osama bin Laden and the Middle-Eastern terrorist group known as al-Qaeda.

Directions: Read the time line. Then answer questions 1 through 4.

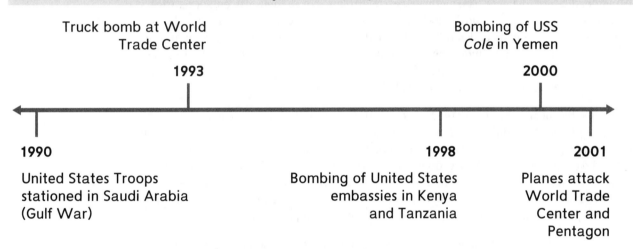

Truck bomb at World
Trade Center

1993

Bombing of USS
Cole in Yemen

2000

1990

United States Troops
stationed in Saudi Arabia
(Gulf War)

1998

Bombing of United States
embassies in Kenya
and Tanzania

2001

Planes attack
World Trade
Center and
Pentagon

1. **Based on the time line, what event led Osama bin Laden to attempt to force Westerners out of the Middle East?**

   A bombing of United States embassies in Kenya and Tanzania

   B United States troops stationed in Saudi Arabia (Gulf War)

   C truck bomb at World Trade Center

   D bombing of USS *Cole* in Yemen

2. **Which event occurred immediately before the terrorist attacks on the World Trade Center and Pentagon?**

   F bombing of United States embassies in Kenya and Tanzania

   G United States Troops stationed in Saudi Arabia (Gulf War)

   H truck bomb at World Trade Center

   J bombing of USS *Cole* in Yemen

3. **Which statement would members of al-Qaeda <u>most likely</u> use to justify the attacks listed in the time line?**

   A Islamic principles should be used to run countries with large Muslim populations.

   B Fundamentalism can be dangerous, but only when it is practiced in Western nations.

   C Westerners are welcome in the Middle East, as long as they remain politically neutral.

   D Only traditional tools and technologies can be used to halt the spread of Western values.

4. **Which event would come next on the time line?**

   F Osama bin Laden assassinated

   G weapons of mass destruction found in Iraq

   H Taliban government overthrown in Afghanistan

   J Saddam Hussein convicted of crimes against humanity

Directions: Read the excerpt. Then answer questions 5 and 6.

Today, our fellow citizens, our way of life, our very freedom came under attack in a series of deliberate and deadly terrorist acts. The victims were in airplanes or in their offices: secretaries, business men and women, military and federal workers, moms and dads, friends and neighbors. Thousands of lives were suddenly ended by evil, despicable acts of terror. The pictures of airplanes flying into buildings, fires burning, huge—huge structures collapsing have filled us with disbelief, terrible sadness, and a quiet, unyielding anger. These acts of mass murder were intended to frighten our nation into chaos and retreat. But they have failed. Our country is strong.

A great people has been moved to defend a great nation. Terrorist attacks can shake the foundations of our biggest buildings, but they cannot touch the foundation of America. These acts shatter steel, but they cannot dent the steel of American resolve. America was targeted for attack because we're the brightest beacon for freedom and opportunity in the world. And no one will keep that light from shining. Today, our nation saw evil—the very worst of human nature—and we responded with the best of America. With the daring of our rescue workers, with the caring for strangers and neighbors who came to give blood and help in any way they could.

—President George W. Bush, Address to the Nation, September 11, 2001

5. **What does President Bush suggest was a main target of the attacks on September 11, 2001?**

   A American commerce

   B American technology

   C American social values

   D American political views

6. **According to Bush, the attack on September 11, 2001, was a terrorist attack. This type of attack is characterized by which strategy?**

   F use of propaganda to incite violence

   G use of violence to frighten opponents

   H use of force to overthrow governments

   J use of demonstrations to protest policies

Directions: Read the question. Then select the correct answer.

7. **President Bush's first response to the attacks of September 11, 2001, was to**

   A invade Iraq

   B put Saddam Hussein on trial

   C assassinate Osama bin Laden

   D launch a war against Afghanistan

The Global War on Terror

In response to the terrorist attacks of 9/11, the United States launched an anti-terrorism campaign that has become known as the global war on terror.

Directions: Study the time line. Then answer questions 8 and 9.

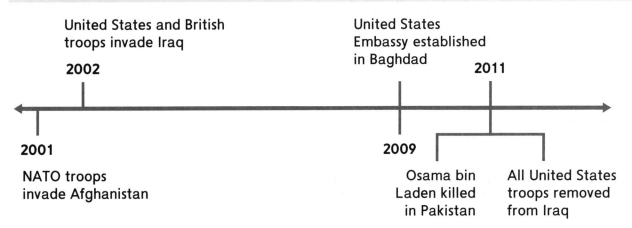

8. **This time line illustrates the effect that the terrorist attacks of 9/11 had on**

   F United States immigration policy

   G United States economic policy

   H United States domestic policy

   J United States foreign policy

9. **Which event on the time line would <u>most likely</u> be opposed by the United Nations?**

   A NATO troops invade Afghanistan

   B all United States troops removed from Iraq

   C United States and British troops invade Iraq

   D United States Embassy established in Baghdad

 **Test-Taking Tip**

When you are drawing a conclusion about a series of events on a time line, try to identify what the different events have in common.

Directions: Read the excerpt. Then answer questions 10 through 13.

(1) North Korea is a regime arming with missiles and weapons of mass destruction, while starving its citizens. (2) Iran aggressively pursues these weapons and exports terror, while an unelected few repress the Iranian people's hope for freedom. (3) Iraq continues to flaunt its hostility toward America and to support terror. (4) The Iraqi regime has plotted to develop anthrax and nerve gas and nuclear weapons for over a decade. (5) This is a regime that has already used poison gas to murder thousands of its own citizens, leaving the bodies of mothers huddled over their dead children. (6) This is a regime that agreed to international inspections then kicked out the inspectors. (7) This is a regime that has something to hide from the civilized world. (8) States like these, and their terrorist allies, constitute an axis of evil, arming to threaten the peace of the world. (9) By seeking weapons of mass destruction, these regimes pose a grave and growing danger. (10) They could provide these arms to terrorists, giving them the means to match their hatred. (11) They could attack our allies or attempt to blackmail the United States. (12) In any of these cases, the price of indifference would be catastrophic.

—President George W. Bush, State of the Union Address, 2002

10. President Bush most likely gave this speech to justify the

   F invasion of Iraq

   G passage of the Patriot Act

   H assassination of Osama bin Laden

   J creation of the Department of Homeland Security

11. Which of the following sentences includes language that is meant to evoke an emotional response in those hearing the speech?

   A sentence 3

   B sentence 5

   C sentence 7

   D sentence 9

12. Which sentence about Iraq includes an unsupported claim that cannot be verified by fact-checking?

   F sentence 4

   G sentence 5

   H sentence 6

   J sentence 7

13. Based on the excerpt, the nations discussed in this speech "constitute an axis of evil" because they

   A are wasting resources that could benefit their people

   B have mistreated international weapons inspectors

   C are developing weapons of mass destruction

   D have directly attacked the United States

This lesson will help you understand the nature of markets and how competition and monopolies affect the economy. Use it with Core Lesson 5.1 *Markets, Competition, and Monopolies* to reinforce and apply your knowledge.

Key Concept

Buyers and sellers exchange goods and services in a market. Monopoly occurs when a business in a market has no competition, but with many businesses, competition can thrive.

Core Skills & Practices

- Predict Outcomes
- Synthesize Ideas from Multiple Sources

Markets

The economy consists of markets in which people and businesses exchange goods and services.

Directions: Read the following questions and choose the best answer.

1. **What is the best definition of *market*?**
   A a type of work that meets a particular need
   B a relationship that makes buying and selling easier
   C a place where services but not goods are provided
   D a process of offering price and quality to gain business

2. **Which of these would be considered a market?**
   F a classroom
   G an aircraft carrier
   H a private golf course
   J a state forest preserve

3. **Why did money begin to take the place of barter in market exchanges?**
   A Money made the exchanges fairer.
   B Money made the exchanges easier.
   C Money made the exchanges more enjoyable.
   D Barter was not possible in market exchanges.

4. **Which outcome is most likely when a video game becomes very popular?**
   F The video game company will cut the price to make the game more popular.
   G The video game company will increase the price of the video game.
   H The company's cost of making the video game rises.
   J The video game company keeps the price the same.

5. Which is <u>most likely</u> to be at a disadvantage in a market economy when resources are scarce?

A business owners who buy the resources

B owners of resources who provide materials for production

C people who do not have enough money to pay for resources

D workers who use resources to make goods or provide services

6. Which company is most likely to offer goods and services?

F auto repair shop

G bookstore

H doctor's office

J florist

Competition

When there is competition in the market, buyers have more choices and more control over how much they have to pay for the goods and services they buy.

Directions: Read the following questions and choose the best answer.

7. Look at the chart below.

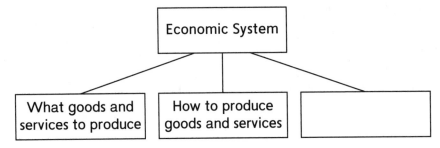

Which statement would fit in the third box?

A why to produce them

B how much to sell them for

C where to get the resources

D for whom to produce them

8. In a market economy, the problem of distribution is largely resolved by

F capitalism

G government

H price

J wages

9. **Read the information in the box.**

> Ben and Sue's Restaurant, in business for 30 years, features all original recipes from Chef Janison; NOW we are hosting live entertainment every Thurs. through Sat. nights; all local musicians. Come and enjoy the atmosphere; and bring a few friends.

The ad is an example of how a business can engage in which of these?

A nonprice competition

B psychological advertising

C service

D specialization

Directions: Read the excerpt. Then answer the questions 10 and 11.

It is not from the benevolence of the butcher, the brewer, or the baker that we expect our dinner, but from their regard to their own interest. We address ourselves, not to their humanity but to their self-love. . . . Give me what I want, and you shall have this which you want, is the meaning of every such offer; and it is the manner that we obtain from one another the far greater part of those good offices which we stand in need of.

—Adam Smith
The Wealth of Nations, 1776

10. **If we need meat for dinner but cannot afford to pay for it, why is it futile to depend on the butcher to provide it for free?**

F The butcher is not motivated to help.

G The butcher is not motivated by benevolence.

H The butcher must compete with the brewer and the baker.

J The butcher wants to be benevolent but can't afford to be.

11. **According to Smith, what roles do benevolence and self-interest have in a transaction?**

A Buyers and sellers are motivated by self-interest.

B Sellers are motivated by self-interest and benevolence.

C Buyers are motivated by benevolence and not self-interest.

D Sellers are motivated by benevolence more than self-interest.

✓ Test-Taking Tip

The text features that you use to determine the sequence of events can also help you find the correct answer in a test passage more quickly. When you first read a passage, make a mental note of any section headings that are used to organize the passage. Later, when you read the questions, notice whether the question tells you where in the passage to look for the answer. If it does, go straight to that section and make sure your answer corresponds to the information found in that section.

Monopolies

The government has enacted several laws to prevent monopolies from forming. There are several kinds of monopolies. Companies often spend large amounts of money in research to develop new products for which they can acquire patents. This gives them the exclusive right to sell the product for many years.

Directions: Read the following questions and choose the best answer.

12. **Which is the most likely behavior of a company that is a monopoly?**
    F It produces a unique product.
    G It invests a lot of money on advertising.
    H It changes its prices based on buyers' desires.
    J It freely shares information about its products.

13. **What kind of law protects technological monopolies?**
    A antitrust law
    B copyright law
    C interstate commerce law
    D patent law

Directions: Look at the chart below. Then answer questions 14 and 15.

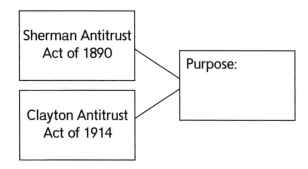

14. **The Sherman and Clayton Antitrust Acts are examples of government action designed to**
    F limit trade
    G keep markets competitive
    H set fair prices for consumers
    J increase the profits of large corporations

15. **What was the purpose of these two acts?**
    A to protect patents
    B to prevent monopolies
    C to interfere with markets
    D to encourage research and development

This lesson will help you understand the four factors of production that make all markets work. Use it with Core Lesson 5.2 *Factors of Production* to reinforce and apply your knowledge.

Key Concept

The factors of production, which include natural resources, labor, capital, and entrepreneurship, are used to produce goods and services.

Core Skills & Practices

- Make Inferences
- Analyze Ideas

Scarcity and Choice

We all have needs and wants, things we must have to survive and other things that we would enjoy having. However, we have a limited amount of money to spend on both. How do we choose?

Directions: Read the following questions. Then select the correct answers.

1. *Scarcity* **is usually understood as the rarity or short supply of something. In economics, however, scarcity depends on two criteria. What are they?**

   A ease of production and price

   B natural resources and cost of goods

   C less supply than demand and the product has value

   D more supply than demand and the product has value

2. **A video game that sold for $49.95 when it was released two years ago now sells for $9.95. What <u>most likely</u> caused this drop in price?**

   F The product was poorly marketed.

   G Production of the game exceeded the demand.

   H High demand for the product drove prices down.

   J The opportunity cost was too high.

3. **Read the information in the box.**

   > Your cell phone has stopped working, and you need to buy a new one. Two models offer the same benefits, but one costs $50.00 more than the other. You wanted to use that $50.00 to take a friend to her favorite restaurant for her birthday. After reading the reviews of both phone models, you choose the more expensive one and decide to make a nice dinner at home for your friend.

   What is the opportunity cost of this decision?

   A taking your friend to a restaurant

   B making her birthday dinner at home

   C getting a better phone for more money

   D spending $50.00 more than you wanted to spend

4. **Which factor of production is the <u>most</u> difficult for business owners to control?**

   F human resources

   G natural resources

   H capital resources

   J entrepreneurship

Natural and Human Resources

Two of the four factors of production involve natural resources and human resources.

Directions: Read the excerpt. Then answer questions 5 through 8.

In the 1830s, Samuel Colt invented the Colt revolver. This gun could be fired six times without reloading. Many people claim that it helped the United States settle the West. Colt had a plan for manufacturing his guns. He explained his idea in a letter to his father:

"The first workman would receive two or three of the most important parts, and would affix these together and pass them on to the next who would do the same, and so on until the complete [revolver] is put together. It would then be inspected and given the finishing touches by experts and each [gun] would be exactly alike and all of its parts would be the same. The workmen, by constant practice in a single operation, would become highly skilled and at the same time very quick and expert at their particular task. So you have better guns and more of them for less money than if you hire men and have each one make the entire [revolver]."

Quoted in *Yankee Arms Maker: The Incredible Career of Samuel Colt,* by Jack Rohan
(Harper & Bros., 1935).

5. **Which <u>best</u> describes how Samuel Colt was an entrepreneur?**

   A He produced each revolver with the same parts.

   B He built a new weapon that fired more efficiently.

   C He hired skilled workers to manufacture weapons.

   D He began a business that used new production methods.

6. **Which factor of production was the main focus of Samuel Colt's idea?**

   F natural resources

   G human resources

   H relative scarcity

   J supply and demand

7. **Why did he think this method would improve productivity?**

   A The workers would take more pride in their work.

   B The value of the product would rise in the market.

   C The quality and the speed of production would increase.

   D The cost of production would be less dependent on natural resources.

8. **How would employment be affected by this method?**

   F More workers would be needed to meet demand.

   G More products could be produced by fewer workers.

   H A shortage of workers would be an ongoing concern.

   J Experienced workers could demand higher wages for their work.

Capital and Entrepreneurship

When you combine capital resources with natural resources and labor, more goods and services can be produced.

Directions: Read the excerpt. Then answer questions 9 through 11.

In 1902 Hershey began producing its famous "KISSES® candy pieces." Each individual KISS® was wrapped by hand. Then in 1921, an invention called a channel wrapper made this labor-intensive part of the process much faster. At the same time, the famous strip of paper—the "plume"—was added. During World War II, the making of KISSES® was put on hold because the silver foil (aluminum) was rationed. Today more than 1,300 KISSES® per minute are produced.

9. **The channel wrapper introduced by the Hershey company is an example of which factor of production?**

   A labor

   B capital resources

   C natural resources

   D production quality

10. **The introduction of the channel wrapper by the Hershey company <u>most directly</u> affected which factor of production?**

    F labor

    G capital resources

    H natural resources

    J production quality

11. **Manufacturers such as Hershey best handle rationing—the regulation of quantities and kinds of goods bought, sold, and traded—by**

    A reducing the labor force

    B stopping production until the rationing is lifted

    C finding alternative natural resources that work well

    D increasing his capital costs by adding new machinery

Directions: Look at the map. Then answer questions 12 and 13

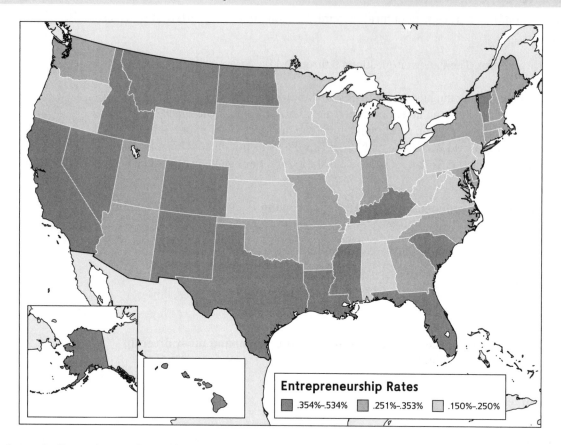

Data shown indicate the number of businesses per 100,000 adults in each state. For example, in 2012 there were 530 businesses per 100,000 people in the state of Montana (rate = 0.53).

12. **States in which automobile manufacturing and mining have been a large part of their economies (Michigan, Ohio, Pennsylvania, Wisconsin, etc.) are shown in the lightest color. Which economic factor probably plays the greatest role in those states having less entrepreneurship than other states?**

   F lack of transportation resources

   G lack of natural resources such as coal, water, or oil

   H lack of appropriately trained labor for new ventures

   J fewer wealthy leaders to provide capital for new businesses

13. **Which state has a high level of entrepreneurship?**

   A Arizona

   B Illinois

   C Minnesota

   D Texas

Test-Taking Tip

Before answering a question about a map, take time to analyze the information show. If there is a map key, make sure you understand what each symbol represents and how the information is related to the map.

This lesson will help you understand how businesses can increase profits and productivity. Use it with Core Lesson 5.3 *Profits and Productivity* to reinforce and apply your knowledge.

Key Concept	Core Skills & Practices
The possibility of increased profits is an incentive for business owners to take risks, expand, and to try various strategies that will increase productivity.	• Interpret Graphics • Use Context Clues to Understand Meaning

Risks and Profits

Starting a new business is risky, but entrepreneurs and workers are willing to take risks in order to make a profit.

Directions: Look at the graph. Then answer questions 1 through 3.

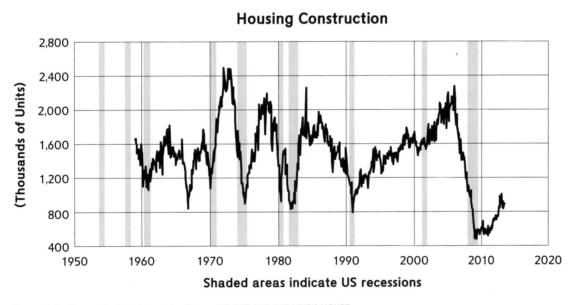

Housing Construction

Shaded areas indicate US recessions

Source: http://research.stlouisfed.org/fred2/graph/?s%5b1%5d%5bid%5d=HOUST

1. **According to the chart, in what year did homebuilders take the fewest risks to start new housing unit?**

   A 1982

   B 1991

   C 2001

   D 2009

2. **Based on data in the chart, what is the <u>greatest</u> risk for a homebuilder?**

   F threat of a recession

   G rising cost of materials

   H declining number of houses on the market

   J period of time that it takes to construct a house

3. **Based on data in the chart, why would 1995 have been a good year to begin a home building business?**

   A demand for new houses was at its highest in 1995

   B more people owned homes than in any other year

   C home prices were lower than they ever had been

   D people were buying houses at an increasing rate

Directions: Read the following questions. Then select the best answer.

4. *Profit* **is the difference between**

   F income from sales and expenses

   G cash on hand and savings

   H income and investments

   J wages and sales

5. **Why do entrepreneurs try to lower their expenses?**

   A to minimize their profit

   B to minimize their risks

   C to minimize their yearly income

   D to minimize the amount of cash on hand

Productivity and Profits

One way that businesses increase profits is through productivity.

Directions: Look at the chart. Then answer questions 6 and 7.

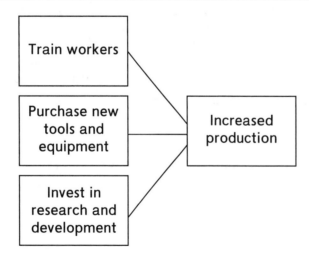

6. **What is the opportunity cost associated with the graphic shown here?**

   F an increase in available capital

   G a temporary increase in output

   H a temporary drop in current production

   J a decrease in goods and an increase in services produced

7. **Which option does not impact productivity?**

   A upgrading technology

   B research and development

   C employee training programs

   D decreasing capital investments

Directions: Look at the table. Then answer questions 8 and 9.

Global Top Ten Firms Spending on Research and Development [billions] [in a recent year]		
Roche Holding	global health care	$9.1
Microsoft software	electronics	$9
Nokia	telecommunications	$8.2
Toyota	automobiles	$7.8
Pfizer	pharmaceuticals	$7.7
Novartis	pharmaceuticals	$7.5
Johnson & Johnson	pharmaceutical	$7
Sanofi Aventis	pharmaceuticals	$6.3
Glaxo Smith Kline	pharmaceuticals	$6.2
Samsung	electronics	$6

Source: *The Christian Science Monitor*

8. **According to the chart, which group of companies spends the most on research and development?**

   F automobiles

   G electronics

   H global healthcare

   J pharmaceuticals

9. **What justifies large expenses for research and development in these or any companies?**

   A rising costs

   B potential earnings

   C the lack of competition

   D the number of people in the market

Directions: Read the following question and choose the best answer.

10. **Land, buildings, and equipment that are used to produce other goods or services are together called**

   F capital resources

   G human resources

   H natural resources

   J production costs

Incentives and Risk Taking

Individuals and businesses are more willing to take risks and invest in their new products if they are encouraged to do so with incentives.

Directions: Read the following questions. Then select the best answers.

11. **Why are there fewer incentives in a traditional economy?**

    A Capital resources are unavailable in a traditional economy.

    B Resources cannot be bought or sold in a traditional economy.

    C Most of the property is privately owned in a traditional economy.

    D There is a high degree of entrepreneurship in a traditional economy.

12. **In the United States, the government has the right to take away a person's property if the government does what?**

    F The government owns the building, so it doesn't have to do anything.

    G If they just take it by force.

    H If they arrest the owner.

    J If they pay the owner.

13. **Today, no modern developed country has which kind of economic system?**

    A command

    B free market

    C mixed

    D traditional

14. **Why is there often a sharp increase in economic growth in a country with a command economy that allows free market incentives?**

    F The government in a country with a command economy forces people to work harder.

    G The government in a country with a command economy is more adaptable to free market conditions.

    H Increased economic freedom and opportunity give people incentives to produce more goods and services.

    J Workers in a command economy cannot adapt to new freedoms because they are used to getting paid no matter how productive they are.

✔ Test-Taking Tip

When taking a test, you might see a detailed image that is associated with a question. When you see something like this on a test, it helps to read the question first to determine exactly what it is asking. Then look at the image with the purpose of gathering only the details that will help you answer the question.

This lesson will help you understand how and why businesses decide what they are going to produce by looking at what other companies produce. Use it with Core Lesson 5.4 *Specialization and Comparative Advantage* to reinforce and apply your knowledge.

Key Concept

Specialization increases productivity and provides businesses with a comparative advantage but also leads to interdependence.

Core Skills & Practices

- Identify Facts and Details
- Gather Information

Specialization

Specialization is when a company decides to focus on making only a few goods or providing a limited number of services. This helps the company become more profitable because it finds ways to be very efficient.

Directions: Read the excerpt. Then answer questions 1 and 2.

With more than a century of growing potatoes, Idaho has produced more than any other state every year since 1957, producing around 30 percent of the US fall production per year. Bingham County produces almost more potatoes than the entire state of Maine! Potatoes contribute more than $2 billion, or approximately 15%, of Idaho's gross state product.

—Idaho State Department of Education

1. **Which statement best describes Idaho's market position in potatoes?**
   A Idaho is the only state that grows potatoes.
   B Idaho potatoes taste better than other varieties.
   C Idaho enjoys an absolute advantage in growing potatoes.
   D Idaho has a higher comparative advantage in growing potatoes.

2. **To produce so many potatoes, farmers in Idaho must be very**
   F efficient
   G opportunistic
   H resourceful
   J thrifty

Directions: Read the questions and choose the best answer.

3. **An *absolute advantage* is the ability to produce a product or service using**
   A different resources than other producers
   B similar resources than other producers
   C fewer resources than other producers
   D more resources than other producers

4 **Look at the chart.**

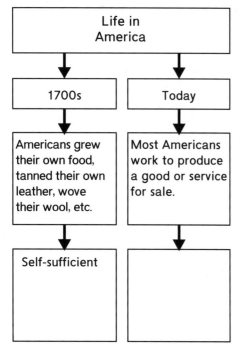

Which word best fits the empty box?

F absolute advantage

G comparative advantage

H opportunity cost

J specialization

Comparative Advantage

Individuals and businesses with a comparative advantage specialize in goods or services that are produced at a relatively low opportunity cost; that is, more easily than other companies could.

Directions: Read the following questions and choose the best answer.

5. **Company A and Company B make mops and brooms. If Company A can make more mops and brooms than Company B, it has**

A a lower absolute advantage

B an equal absolute advantage

C a higher absolute advantage

D a comparative absolute advantage

6. **The law of comparative advantage says that those with the lower opportunity cost should**

   F produce both goods

   G seek an absolute advantage

   H produce fewer goods or services

   J specialize in that product or service

Directions: Study the graph. Then answer questions 7 through 9.

Production of Guns and Butter

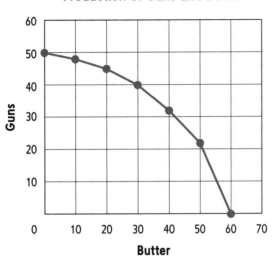

7. **How many guns could be produced if no butter is produced?**

   A 50

   B 60

   C 70

   D 80

8. **If the same producer made guns and butter, what is the maximum number of both items that could be produced?**

   F 45

   G 60

   H 75

   J 110

9. **By specializing and producing the item for which he has a comparative advantage, a gun producer could produce a maximum of**

   A 50 guns

   B 60 guns

   C 70 guns

   D 130 guns

10. By specializing and producing those items for which they had a comparative advantage, a separate gun producer and butter producer could together have a combined production possibility of

F 60 guns + 50 butter

G 50 guns + 60 butter

H 60 guns + 70 butter

J 70 guns + 60 butter

Interdependence

When businesses are linked to other businesses to operate, they are said to be interdependent.

Directions: Read the following questions. Then select the correct answers.

11. When producers are interdependent, what do they share?

A costs

B productivity

C profits

D resources

12. What benefits would help a producer minimize the risk that interdependence poses?

F Decreased specialization results in increased trade.

G Increased profitability results from increased trade.

H Decreased profitability results in decreased competition.

J Increased specialization results in increased productivity.

13. When two countries are interdependent, which of these statements is true?

A Both countries can afford to not specialize.

B Both countries will see a rise in productivity.

C Negative economic events in one country have little effect in the other.

D The countries are more likely to trade with other countries than with one another.

14. Which of the following situations is a disadvantage for a car manufacturer that is dependent on tires supplied by a company in another country?

F The other country starts producing its own cars.

G A competing car manufacturer goes out of business.

H The car manufacturer's country puts a limit on imported cars.

J The rubber industry workers in the other country go on strike.

✔ Test-Taking Tip

When reading multiple-choice questions, look for superlatives, such as *always* or *best*. These indicate that the correct answer has to be a very precise fact that can never be disputed. Very few answers will fit that criteria.

This lesson will help you understand how the economic behavior of individuals and companies can be analyzed. Use it with Core Lesson 6.1 *Microeconomics* to reinforce and apply your knowledge.

Key Concept

The forces of supply and demand determine the market prices of most products and resources in the United States and global economies.

Core Skills & Practices

- Interpreting Charts, and Graphs
- Analyze Information

Market Influences

The forces of supply and demand on the market influence local and national economies.

Directions: Read the following questions and choose the best answer.

1. **In a market economy, which one of these options influences the supply side of the market?**
   - **A** buyers
   - **B** consumers
   - **C** government
   - **D** producers

2. **In a mixed economy,**
   - **F** the economy is centrally planned
   - **G** the forces of supply and demand have very little influence
   - **H** the government regulates the economy while allowing market forces to work
   - **J** the government sets prices and controls the quantities of goods and services that are in the market

3. **Which statement best describes how prices are set?**
   - **A** Sellers set prices for goods and services.
   - **B** Buyers set prices for goods and services.
   - **C** Manufacturers set prices for goods and services.
   - **D** Sellers set prices, but buyers influence price changes.

4. **What is the most likely effect of a product rising in price?**
   - **F** Producers make a different product.
   - **G** Consumers buy more of the product.
   - **H** Producers increase production of the product.
   - **J** Producers decrease production of the product.

Laws of Supply and Demand

Supply (the amount of goods and services available) and demand (how much consumers desire a product) are two concepts that are related in a free market economy.

Directions: Study the graph. Then answer questions 5 through 7.

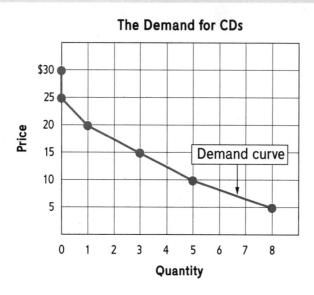

5. **Between which two prices did market demand increase the most?**

    A $25.00 and $20.00

    B $20.00 and $15.00

    C $15.00 and $10.00

    D $10.00 and $5.00

6. **How many CDs would be demanded at a price of $15.00?**

    F 3

    G 5

    H 8

    J 10

7. **What does a demand curve tell you about the relationship between the price of a good and the quantity of that good?**

    A As quantity increases, price increases.

    B As quantity decreases, price decreases.

    C As the price rises, the quantity increases.

    D As the price decreases, the quantity increases.

8. **Look at the graph.**

Price of 40″ LED Televisions

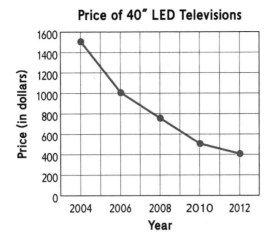

The price of televisions is decreasing over time, which is shown by which aspect of the graph?

F   the equilibrium

G   the median

H   the supply

J   the trend

9. **If the price rises, the quantity supplied also rises. If the price drops, the quantity supplied goes down as well. What explains this?**

A   Sales generate more business.

B   People do not usually buy in bulk.

C   The profit motive drives suppliers.

D   Prices are not always a good signal.

10. **What does a supply curve tell you about the relationship between supply and price?**

F   As quantity decreases, price rises.

G   As quantity increases, price increases.

H   As the price rises, the quantity decreases.

J   As price decreases, the quantity increases.

Market Equilibrium

The aim of the market is to compromise between the interests of the buyers and the interests of the sellers, a term called market equilibrium, which is reached when demand is equal to the supply.

Directions: Study the graph. Then answer the questions 11 through 13.

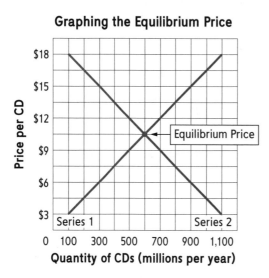

Graphing the Equilibrium Price

11. **The equilibrium price is where the quantity demanded meets the**
    A price supplied
    B price demanded
    C supply demanded
    D quantity supplied

12. **According to this graph, what is the equilibrium price and how many CDs will be sold at that price?**
    F $10.00/100 million
    G $10.00/600 million
    H $15.00/800 million
    J $20.00/1.1 billion

13. **For Series 1, how many CDs are sold at $15.00?**
    A 700
    B 800
    C 900
    D 1,000

This lesson will help you understand how our government forms and carries out policies that affect the nation's economy. Use it with Core Lesson 6.2 *Macroeconomics and Government Policy* to reinforce and apply your knowledge.

Key Concept

The federal government uses fiscal policies and monetary policies to manage the economy.

Core Skills & Practices

- Identify Comparisons and Contrasts
- Interpret Meaning

Federal Revenue and Expenditures

The federal government collects income, mostly from taxes, so it is able to perform its business.

Directions: Read the following questions and choose the best answer.

1. **Approximately half of the government's income, or *revenue*, comes from**
   A tariffs
   B user fees
   C income taxes
   D property taxes

2. **What must the federal government do to collect revenue to pay for its budget deficit?**
   F borrow money
   G pay off its bonds
   H collect import tariffs
   J collect income taxes

3. **How does the government borrow money from American citizens?**
   A collecting income taxes
   B placing tariffs on imports
   C selling bonds to individuals
   D collecting Medicare payroll deductions

4. **Government expenditures can be defined as**
   F taxes, tariffs, and fees
   G money that the government pays out
   H revenue that the government takes in
   J the difference between revenue and expenses

Directions: Look at the graph. Then answer questions 5 through 7.

Fiscal Year 2011 Budget Request

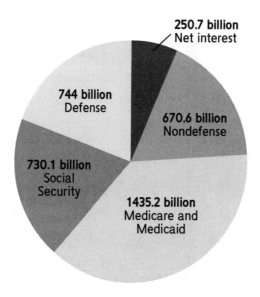

250.7 billion
Net interest

744 billion
Defense

670.6 billion
Nondefense

730.1 billion
Social
Security

1435.2 billion
Medicare and
Medicaid

5. **According to the graph, what was most of the 2011 federal budget devoted to?**
   A Defense
   B Medicare and Medicaid
   C Net interest
   D Social Security

6 **Which two portions of the budget account for almost equal amounts?**
   F Defense and Medicare
   G Net interest and Nondefense
   H Defense and Social Security
   J Social Security and Net interest

7 **What do you think could cause the Net Interest to decrease?**
   A a decrease in the federal deficit
   B an increase in Nondefense spending
   C a rise in Defense spending due to war
   D a decrease in the number of people eligible for Social Security benefits

 **Test-Taking Tip**

Read the title of a circle graph to identify the topic. Look for labels to explain
what the different slices represent.

Federal Fiscal and Monetary Policies

To manage its economy effectively, the federal government has specific plans and laws related to money supply, credit, and interest rates.

Directions: Read the following questions and choose the best answer.

8. Which is <u>most likely</u> to be taxed at the lowest rate?

    F alcohol

    G cigarettes

    H energy-efficient products

    J gasoline

9. How are quotas and tariffs similar?

    A Both raise revenue for the government.

    B Both put limits on imported goods.

    C Both increase foreign competition.

    D Both discourage local production.

10. What have <u>most recent</u> government subsidies been created to do?

    F balance the national budget

    G lower the cost of food products

    H provide aid for the unemployed

    J construct new bridges and roads

11. How can federal regulations have a negative effect on the economy?

    A by limiting monopolies and encouraging competition

    B by making products more expensive to manufacture

    C by discouraging efficiency and promoting waste

    D by outlawing unfair trade and pricing practices

12. During good economic times, the Federal Reserve will pursue policies designed to

    F regulate financial institutions as little as possible

    G reduce interest rates as low as possible

    H control inflation as much as possible

    J increase liquidity when available

13. How might a subsidy on corn affect consumers?

    A It would increase the cost of corn to consumers.

    B It would reduce the cost of corn to consumers.

    C It would affect the quality of the corn.

    D It would decrease the supply of corn.

Directions: Read the excerpt. Then answer questions 14 and 15.

"In short, the original goal of the Great Experiment that was the founding of the Fed was the preservation of financial stability . . . How should a central bank enhance financial stability? One means is by assuming the lender-of-last-resort function . . . under which the central bank uses its power to provide liquidity to ease market conditions during periods of panic or incipient panic . . . However, putting out the fire is not enough; it is also important to foster a financial system that is sufficiently resilient to withstand large financial shocks. Toward that end, the Federal Reserve, together with other regulatory agencies . . . is actively engaged in monitoring financial developments and working to strengthen financial institutions and markets . . . What about the monetary policy framework? In general, the Federal Reserve's policy framework . . . include[s an] emphasis on preserving the Fed's inflation credibility, which is critical for anchoring inflation expectation."

—Chairman Ben S. Bernanke at "The First 100 Years of the Federal Reserve: The Policy Record, Lessons Learned, and Prospects for the Future," a conference sponsored by the National Bureau of Economic Research, Cambridge, Massachusetts, July 10, 2013

14. **According to the excerpt, what is the primary goal of the Federal Reserve?**

    F to prevent inflation

    G to control the nation's banks

    H to preserve financial stability

    J to monitor fiscal developments

15. **Based on the excerpt, what is meant by the Federal Reserve's "power of liquidity"?**

    A its large number of reserve banks

    B its ability to control the money supply

    C its desire to keep the government stable

    D its independence from the federal government

Directions: Read the following questions and choose the best answer.

16. **Which of these can cause market failures?**

    F bank closings because of panics

    G imperfect competition

    H wrong Fed decisions

    J antitrust acts

17. **What was the intent of the Clayton Antitrust Act of 1914?**

    A to stabilize the economy

    B to enhance competition

    C to subsidize producers

    D to protect consumers

This lesson will help you understand how a variety of practices help measure the health of an economy. Use it with Core Lesson 6.3 *Macroeconomics, the GDP, and Price Fluctuation* to reinforce and apply your knowledge.

Key Concept

Measures such as an economy's GDP, inflation or deflation rate, and unemployment rate provide economists with ways to measure an economy's health.

Core Skills & Practices

• Read Charts
• Integrate Visual Information

Gross Domestic Product

Gross domestic product, the value of all goods and services produced in the nation in a year, is one of the most vital measurements of a nation's economy.

Directions: Read the questions and choose the best answers.

1. **A country's gross domestic product (GDP) is determined by**
   A adding the quantity of goods and services to intermediate goods and services
   B subtracting quantity of goods and services from government spending
   C adding domestic goods and services to imported goods and services
   D multiplying the quantity of goods and services by their prices

2. **In which of these countries would GDP be the least useful measure of the strength of the economy?**
   F an island nation, where bartering is common
   G a large Asian nation with a strong government
   H a tiny nation that is part of the European Union
   J a nation that participates in United States trade agreements

3. **What aspect of GDP is misleading as a measure of nation's overall well-being?**
   A GDP includes economic activity outside of organized markets.
   B GDP includes negative events such as wars and natural disasters.
   C GDP includes the value of goods and services from foreign countries.
   D GDP includes the value of intermediate goods, which results in unreliable figures.

4. **Which of the following products would count toward United States GDP?**
   F California surfboards sold in Mexico
   G natural gas from Canada used in Illinois
   H seats made in Poland, to be installed in a new car in Detroit
   J new American-made tires for an American-made motorcycle

5. **Look at the graph.**

**GDP of Selected
Countries, 2012**

Country	GDP in 2012 (in trillion $)
Canada	1.8
China	8.4
Mexico	1.2
United Kingdom	2.4
United States	15.7

Which country has a GDP that is approximately twice the GDP of Mexico?

A Canada

B China

C United Kingdom

D United States

6. **To help them identify and evaluate economic trends, economists calculate a country's GDP**

F annually

G daily

H monthly

J quarterly

Inflation and Deflation

Inflation and deflation can affect the GDP. As prices rise, the purchasing power of the dollar declines. As prices fall, the purchasing power of the dollar increases.

Directions: Read the following question and choose the best answer.

7. **The term that is used to describe a rise in the general level of prices over time is**

A deflation

B inflation

C integration

D stagflation

 Test-Taking Tip

In multiple-choice questions, if two answers contradict each other, one of them is likely to be the correct answer.

Directions: Study the graph. Then answer questions 8 through 10.

Price of a Market Basket of Goods 1913 to 2013

8. If a person paid $10.00 for a market basket of goods in 1913, how much would the same goods cost in 1983?

   F $30.00

   G $53.00

   H $98.00

   J $230.00

9. The graph is a visual representation of inflation and deflation in the United States economy. During which of these years was there a period of deflation in the United States?

   A 1923

   B 1933

   C 1943

   D 1953

10. The Federal Reserve believes that 2 percent inflation is desirable. At that rate, approximately how much would this market basket of goods <u>most likely</u> cost in 2023?

   F $234.00

   G $245.00

   H $268.00

   J $280.00

Unemployment

Unemployment occurs when people leave their former jobs for any number of reasons and have not yet found new jobs.

Directions: Study the graph. Then answer questions 11 through 13.

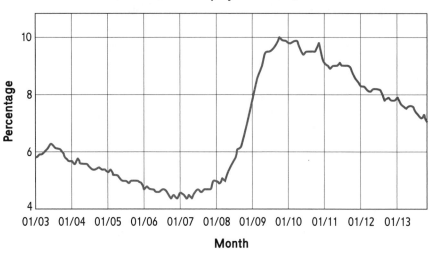

United States Unemployment Rate, 2003–2013

Source: http://data.bls.gov/timeseries/LNS14000000

11. **During which year represented in the graph was the United States unemployment rate highest?**

   A 2008

   B 2009

   C 2010

   D 2012

12. **What was the approximate difference in unemployment rate between the beginning of 2003 and the beginning of 2013?**

   F + 2 percent

   G + 4 percent

   H – 1 percent

   J – 2 percent

13 **The graph is a visual representation of inflation and deflation in the American economy. During which of these years was there a period of deflation in the United States?**

   A 1923

   B 1933

   C 1943

   D 1953

This lesson will help you understand major economic events in US history. Use it with Core Lesson 7.1 *Major Economic Events* to reinforce and apply your knowledge.

Key Concept

The federal government has responded to economic events in a variety of ways, for example, by developing stimulus programs and regulating businesses.

Core Skills & Practices

- Analyze Information
- Identify Point of View

Booms and Busts

Throughout its history, the United States has experienced economic booms and busts.

Directions: Read the following questions and choose the best answer.

1. **How can inflation weaken an economy?**
   - **A** It leads companies to increase production, shrinking demand.
   - **B** It causes stocks bought on margin to drop in value.
   - **C** It causes people to buy luxuries they cannot afford.
   - **D** It reduces demand for goods, shrinking GDP.

2. **Mass production had what effect on the economy in the 1920s?**
   - **F** It lowered the prices of goods significantly.
   - **G** It caused the unemployment rate to increase.
   - **H** It caused a trough to develop in the economy.
   - **J** It allowed an increase in middle class families.

3. **At a certain point, an increased demand for Model Ts would lead to a drop in supply. At that point, which of these is likely to have happened?**
   - **A** a decrease in inflation
   - **B** an economic trough
   - **C** an increase in price
   - **D** a decline in GDP

4. **The years 1920 to 1929 in the United States would be considered a time of**
   - **F** recession
   - **G** economic boom
   - **H** decrease in GDP
   - **J** increased federal spending

The Great Depression

The Great Depression was a period of severe decline in the United States economy during the 1930s.

Directions: Read the following questions and choose the best answer.

5. **Why did the Stock Market continue to drop during October, 1929?**

   A Production in factories in the United States had hit its peak.

   B Investors panicked and sold their stocks.

   C People bought cheap stocks on margin.

   D People had little faith in banks.

6. **What is the most likely reason Hoovervilles would have persisted beyond the Great Depression?**

   F Strong communities were formed in these shantytowns.

   G Some Hooverville governments were highly effective.

   H Some people preferred living outside to living inside.

   J Relief programs took time to help all those in need.

Directions: Read the excerpt. Then answer questions 7 and 8.

During the period between 1929 and 1933, over 100,000 businesses failed, causing massive job loss. Without employment, many families lost their homes. With almost 25 percent of American workers out of work and homeless, shantytowns began to appear in parks and at the edges of cities. These collections of shacks were called "Hoovervilles." Although Hoovervilles were made of temporary and makeshift structures, some were organized, with a mayor and governing committees. Even after the Great Depression, Hoovervilles persisted in some areas.

7. **Why were the shantytowns named Hoovervilles?**

   A Massive unemployment and foreclosures occurred during President Hoover's tenure as president.

   B President Hoover had been involved in the stock market crash, which had damaged the US economy.

   C President Hoover had enacted many government programs that provided economic relief to individuals.

   D Many companies owned by President Hoover had failed, increasing unemployment during the Great Depression.

8. **What is the most likely reason that shantytowns were located in parks and at the edges of cities?**

   F Building materials were more abundant there.

   G Foreclosed homes were usually near these areas.

   H These areas were a source of public or unused land.

   J Cities set aside these areas for the homeless and poor.

The Government Responds

The federal government implemented laws and set up agencies to combat economic hardship and to pull the United States out of the Great Depression.

Directions: Read the following questions and choose the best answer.

9. **Which definition fits the meaning of the term *stimulus*?**

    A a period of time when the country's GDP grows

    B a dramatic increase in the price of goods and services

    C government policies to provide relief to workers and businesses

    D a system in which the means of production are controlled by the government

10. **Why did President Herbert Hoover not take steps to address the Great Depression in its early years?**

    F He was worried that if he acted too aggressively it would hurt his chances for reelection.

    G He feared that too much government involvement amounted to socialism.

    H He tried to work out a joint response with state governments.

    J He was too involved in addressing foreign crises.

11. **Why did farmers choose to destroy their crops in the early 1930s?**

    A They thought the increase in supply would lower demand and people would pay more.

    B They thought the shortage would lead to higher demand and prices would go up.

    C They thought they could create a surplus and people would buy more food.

    D They thought this would lower costs, encouraging people to buy more.

✅ Test-Taking Tip

When trying to determine the correct answer to a multiple-choice question, begin by deciding the correct answer before looking at the answer choices. Then, match the answer you believe to be correct with one of the possible choices.

Directions: Read the excerpt. Then answer questions 12 through 14.

(1) Our greatest primary task is to put people to work. (2) This is no unsolvable problem if we face it wisely and courageously. (3) It can be accomplished in part by direct recruiting by the Government itself, treating the task as we would treat the emergency of a war, but at the same time, through this employment, accomplishing greatly needed projects to stimulate and reorganize the use of our natural resources. . . (4) The task can be helped by definite efforts to raise the values of agricultural products and with this the power to purchase the output of our cities. (5) It can be helped by preventing realistically the tragedy of the growing loss through foreclosure of our small homes and our farms. (6) It can be helped by insistence that the Federal, State, and local governments act forthwith on the demand that their cost be drastically reduced. (7) It can be helped by the unifying of relief activities which today are often scattered, uneconomical, and unequal. (8) It can be helped by national planning for and supervision of all forms of transportation and of communications and other utilities which have a definitely public character. (9) There are many ways in which it can be helped, but it can never be helped merely by talking about it. (10) We must act and act quickly.

—President Franklin D. Roosevelt, First Inaugural Address, 1933

12. **The issue Roosevelt discusses in sentence 4 of this passage was <u>most directly</u> addressed by which government agency?**

  F Tennessee Valley Authority

  G Civilian Conservation Corps

  H Works Progress Administration

  J Agricultural Adjustment Administration

13. **In which sentence does Roosevelt speak of an issue that would be partially addressed by the creation of Social Security?**

  A sentence 4

  B sentence 5

  C sentence 7

  D sentence 8

14. **Which of these statements summarizes Roosevelt's point of view, as outlined in his speech?**

  F Local and state governments are corrupt and must be reined in.

  G The economy can be improved through government intervention.

  H The government must control all aspects of the American economy.

  J Direct monetary relief is the only way to help the poorest Americans.

This lesson will help you understand the relationship between political and economic freedoms, identify the economic causes and impacts of wars, and discuss how exploration and colonization were driven by economic factors. Use it with Core Lesson 7.2 *The Relationship Between Politics and Economics* to reinforce and apply your knowledge.

Key Concept

Politics and economics interact with each other in complex ways that affect the entire society.

Core Skills & Practices

• Compare and Contrast
• Make Inferences

Political and Economic Freedom

In the United States, the balance between personal freedom, as outlined in the Constitution, and economic freedom is frequently addressed.

Directions: Read the excerpt. Then answer questions 1 through 3.

The time is arriving when we can have further tax reduction, when, unless we wish to hamper the people in their right to earn a living, we must have tax reform. The method of raising revenue ought not to impede the transaction of business; it ought to encourage it. I am opposed to extremely high rates, because they produce little or no revenue, because they are bad for the country, and, finally, because they are wrong. We cannot finance the country, we cannot improve social conditions, through any system of injustice, even if we attempt to inflict it upon the rich. Those who suffer the most harm will be the poor. This country believes in prosperity. It is absurd to suppose that it is envious of those who are already prosperous. The wise and correct course to follow in taxation and all other economic legislation is not to destroy those who have already secured success but to create conditions under which everyone will have a better chance to be successful.

—President Calvin Coolidge, Inaugural Address, 1925

1. **Based on this speech, what approach did President Calvin Coolidge take toward the nation's economic affairs?**

    A centrally planned

    B expansionist

    C Keynesian

    D laissez-faire

2. **Which of these statements does the speech appear to support?**

    F The poor will benefit most from larger taxes on the rich.

    G Prosperity cannot be attained unless taxation is increased.

    H Successful people should not be punished through taxation.

    J The tax system should be completely abolished in the United States.

3. **Which statement is an inference about Coolidge's beliefs that can be made from this speech?**

    A Rich people earned their success.

    B Taxation is completely unnecessary.

    C Poor people have been treated justly.

    D Poor people are jealous of rich people.

Directions: Read the questions and choose the best answer.

4. **President Franklin Roosevelt's economic policy differed from President Coolidge's approach in that Roosevelt**

    F promoted limited government intervention in economic affairs

    G set the ground rules for free enterprise and then left the market alone

    H favored a redistribution of wealth in which personal fortunes would be limited

    J created government programs to put people to work and to stimulate the economy

5. **In the late 1800s, the United States began looking for new markets for goods produced. Why did the government look for new markets?**

    A The United States wanted to become a major world power.

    B The United States produced more goods than Americans could buy.

    C The United States wanted to gain political influence over other nations.

    D The United States needed to form defensive alliances in other parts of the world.

6. **When war occurs in a country, which of these is a common economic effect for its citizens?**

    F a surplus of goods

    G a decrease in jobs

    H a decline in poverty

    J an increase in resources

 Test-Taking Tip

An inference is a conclusion that is reached on the basis of evidence and reasoning. When you are asked to identify an inference based on evidence from a reading passage, first read the inferences that are provided. Then read the passage to see which inference could be made based on information in the passage.

The Politics of Imperialism

The policy of imperialism—the governing of weaker nations or colonies by more powerful nations—is an example of the influence of politics on the economy.

Directions: Read the questions and choose the best answer.

7. **Which statement is an example of a tariff?**
   A The United States and Mexico have the right to trade with China.
   B Hawaii was added to the United States as a territory in 1898.
   C Sugar from Brazil is taxed when it enters the United States.
   D The United States obtained land to build a canal in Panama.

8. **Which definition best fits the meaning of the term *annexation*?**
   F One country takes control of another country or territory.
   G One country offers military support to a weaker neighbor.
   H A territory is transferred from one power to another by treaty.
   J Two countries have a mutually beneficial trading relationship.

Directions: Read the excerpt. Then answer questions 9 and 10.

I, Liliuokalani of Hawaii, by the will of God named heir apparent on the tenth day of April, A.D. 1877, and by the grace of God Queen of the Hawaiian Islands on the seventeenth day of January, A.D. 1893, do hereby protest against the ratification of a certain treaty, which, so I am informed, has been signed at Washington by Messrs. Hatch, Thurston, and Kinney, purporting to cede those Islands to the territory and dominion of the United States. I declare such a treaty to be an act of wrong toward the native and part-native people of Hawaii, an invasion of the rights of the ruling chiefs, in violation of international rights both toward my people and toward friendly nations with whom they have made treaties, the perpetuation of the fraud whereby the constitutional government was overthrown, and, finally, an act of gross injustice to me.

—Queen Liliuokalani of Hawaii, Official Protest to the Treaty of Annexation, 1897

9. **What does Queen Liliuokalani imply about her role as ruler of Hawaii?**
   A She was ordained by God to rule.
   B She was chosen by the people to rule.
   C She supports American rule of Hawaii.
   D She needs help from the United States government.

10. **Why does Queen Liliuokalani protest the treaty referred to in the passage?**
    F It spreads imperialism into the South Pacific region.
    G It overthrows the constitutional government of Hawaii.
    H It gives native Hawaiians more say in their government.
    J It ignores the right of Hawaii to rule itself independently.

The Economics of War

War and economics are interconnected.

Directions: Read the questions and choose the best answer.

11. **Which of these impacts of war could indirectly cause homelessness?**

    A War disrupts businesses.

    B Bombing destroys houses.

    C Fighting destroys farm fields.

    D Conflict shuts down power grids.

12. **In 2011, a revolution in Egypt led the country's longtime dictator to step down. How did foreign investors most likely react to this news?**

    F They saw potential for selling supplies and services to the military.

    G They cancelled plans to do business in Egypt, citing political instability.

    H They seized the opportunity to build business ties with a new government.

    J They urged their governments to provide aid to stabilize Egypt's economy.

Directions: Read the excerpt. Then answer questions 13 and 14.

The United States has a long history of extending a helping hand to people overseas struggling to make a better life. It is a history that both reflects the American people's compassion and support of human dignity as well as advances US foreign policy interests.

—US Agency for International Development, Statement of "Who We Are"

13. **To improve the lives of people in foreign countries that may have been affected by war or famine, the United States often provides**

    A military aid

    B foreign donors

    C humanitarian aid

    D policy initiatives

14. **How would aid from the United States advance United States foreign policy interests?**

    F by stabilizing economies of foreign countries

    G by providing military support to foreign countries

    H by supporting those who want to overthrow dictators

    J by showing that United States citizens can be compassionate

This lesson will help you understand how the Scientific and Industrial Revolutions have shaped modern life. Use it with Core Lesson 7.3 *The Scientific and Industrial Revolutions* to reinforce and apply your knowledge.

Key Concept

Today's world has been shaped by the technological advances that came about as a result of the Scientific and Industrial Revolutions.

Core Skills & Practices

- Interpret Meaning
- Identify Cause and Effect

The Scientific Revolution

During the Scientific Revolution, which lasted from the late 1500s to the early 1600s, people began to use rational thinking to question old ideas about the world around them and to search for new answers.

Directions: Read the questions and choose the best answer.

1. **The series of experiments and observations scientists use to arrive at their conclusions is called**

   A innovation

   B technology

   C the scientific method

   D the process of elimination

2. **Which of these statements <u>best</u> applies to the period of the Scientific Revolution?**

   F Political revolution led to scientific discoveries in many nations.

   G A mass movement of people occurred from the country to cities.

   H Scientists began to accept discoveries that were made in the past.

   J The use of rational thinking caused many old ideas to be discarded.

3. **Which scientist made discoveries related to the human body?**

   A Antonie van Leeuwenhoek

   B Galileo Galilei

   C Isaac Newton

   D Nicholas Copernicus

Directions: Read the excerpt. Then answer questions 4 and 5.

The astrolabe is an instrument that allows the user to study the position of the Sun and stars to determine time during the day or night and the time of a celestial event. During the 15th and 16th century, the Mariner's Astrolabe was developed to measure the height of a celestial body above the horizon.

4. **Which measurement would an astrolabe allow a navigator to determine while sailing in the middle of an ocean?**
   F   distance to land
   G   latitude position
   H   time until sunrise
   J   distance between stars

5. **The invention of the astrolabe had the greatest effect on which of the following?**
   A   industrialization
   B   European exploration
   C   the Scientific Revolution
   D   the work of Copernicus and Galileo

The Industrial Revolution

During the time period known as the Industrial Revolution, machines replaced hand tools in the manufacturing of goods, and many people left their farms to work in factories.

Directions: Read the questions and choose the best answer.

6. **What is the most likely effect of an industrial revolution in a country?**
   F   More people are able to work at home.
   G   People move from the cities to rural areas.
   H   The economy shifts from agriculture to manufacturing.
   J   New machines make more expensive goods that are difficult to obtain.

7. **Why did inventions like the flying shuttle and the spinning machine lead to the end of the cottage industry system?**
   A   People were not needed to run these machines.
   B   The machines were dangerous for children to operate.
   C   Government regulations prohibited families from owning these machines.
   D   The machines were too large and complex to be operated in private homes.

8. **How did India contribute to Britain's success in becoming an industrial society?**
   F   It provided iron to make machines.
   G   It provided coal to run steam engines.
   H   It provided raw cotton for the textile mills.
   J   It provided people to work in manufacturing.

Cotton Mills in England, 1838

Location in England	Number of Cotton Mills	Number of Employees
Northwest	1,562	215,556
Northeast	16	1,704
Southwest	1	29
Southeast	19	942

9. The movement of people from farms to industrial cities appears to have been greatest in which region of England?

   A northeast

   B northwest

   C southeast

   D southwest

10. Based on the information in the chart, you can conclude that in the first half of the 19th century, northwest England most likely developed a higher concentration of

   F middle-class families

   G labor unions

   H universities

   J railroads

11. Based on the information in the chart, you can conclude that any goods produced in the southwest during this period were most likely the result of

   A cottage industries

   B large factories

   C entrepreneurs

   D labor unions

 Test-Taking Tip

When you are answering questions based on a data table, study the table to determine any trends in the data.

The Rise of Cities

Between 1800 and 1850 there was a significant increase in the number and size of cities in Europe and the United States.

Directions: Read the questions and choose the best answer.

12. **What led to urbanization during the Industrial Revolution?**
    - F   the need for factory workers
    - G   the abundance of city services
    - H   healthy living conditions in the cities
    - J   high pay and safe working conditions in city jobs

13. **Before labor unions formed during the Industrial Revolution, which of these statements was true?**
    - A   Employers operated according to their company's set of rules.
    - B   Employers were held responsible for workplace accidents.
    - C   Employee wages were based on experience and gender.
    - D   Employees working long hours received overtime pay.

Directions: Read the excerpt. Then answer questions 14 and 15.

Textile factories in England used child labor to perform many tasks, such as picking up loose cotton or crawling under machines while they were in motion. Interviews with people who worked in cotton mills as children reveal that they were sometimes forced to work from 12 to 17 hours at the mill, and were punished if they tried to sit down or rest in any way. Very small children were sought for mill work, because they were cheaper to hire as well as small and agile.

14. **Which of these jobs in a cotton mill would <u>most likely</u> be done by the youngest or smallest children?**
    - F   running errands for managers
    - G   picking up cotton from the floor
    - H   cleaning cloth-making machinery
    - J   crawling under running machines

15. **Based on the excerpt, which statement <u>best</u> describes conditions during the Industrial Revolution?**
    - A   Education was valued.
    - B   Children were valued.
    - C   Poverty was common.
    - D   Illness was common.

This lesson will help you learn what banks do and how you can use them. Use it with Core Lesson 8.1 *Savings and Banking* to reinforce and apply your knowledge.

Key Concept	**Core Skills & Practices**
Financial institutions provide consumers with services such as checking and savings accounts to help them manage their money.	• Analyze Events and Details • Get Meaning from Context

Banks

Banks are in business to make a profit. They do that by providing three basic services—keeping money safe, transferring funds, and loaning money.

Directions: Read the questions and choose the best answer.

1. **Read the chart.**

Acceptable Ways to Transfer Money from Banks
?
automatic withdrawals for bill payment
checking accounts

   Which method of transferring money best completes the table?

   A savings accounts

   B safe deposit boxes

   C electronic funds transfer

   D sending cash through insured mail

2. **Read the statement in the box.**

   > The National Equity Bank has announced that it has more than $450 billion in cash reserves.

   By making this announcement regarding its cash reserves, the National Equity Bank is advertising its ability to

   F cover depositors' withdrawals

   G purchase competing banks

   H pay interest on debts

   J offer loans

Types of Banks

Over time, several types of banking institutions arose to serve specific needs. Today most financial institutions serve all those needs.

Directions: Read the questions and choose the best answer.

3. **What was the original purpose of a credit union?**
    A to help individuals buy homes
    B to serve the needs of businesses
    C to provide commercial accounts
    D to serve its members with emergency loans

4. **What trend has affected the initial purpose of different financial institutions?**
    F Most financial institutions today offer the same services.
    G Credit unions require members to live in the same community.
    H Savings and loans provide the most money for new home buyers.
    J Commercial banks outnumber all other financial institutions combined.

5. **Consumers generally trust that their banks will not lose their money because**
    A banks have unlimited resources
    B banks buy insurance to cover losses
    C consumers know their local bankers
    D consumers are uninformed about their deposits

6. **Read the chart.**

Thrift Institutions
savings banks
credit unions
?

Which of the following best completes the table?
    F commercial banks
    G insurance companies
    H credit card companies
    J savings and loan associations

Personal Banking

Your bank not only offers to protect your money; it offers many services, for some of which it will charge a fee.

Directions: Read the questions and choose the best answer.

7. **If you have a personal checking account, you can**
   - **A** pay bills late
   - **B** earn a large amount of interest
   - **C** have someone write a check using your name
   - **D** withdraw money by writing a check or using an ATM

8. **Why is it important to keep track of the account balance in your checking account?**
   - **F** to let the bank know how much money is in your account
   - **G** to avoid having your account temporarily closed by the bank
   - **H** to avoid a penalty fee for writing a check for more than the balance
   - **J** to make certain that the bank has enough insurance to cover the balance of your account

9. **Every reputable bank is required to**
   - **A** publicize consumer account information
   - **B** protect consumer privacy
   - **C** offer savings incentives
   - **D** offer free checking

10. **When you write a check for more than the balance in your checking account, the bank will <u>most likely</u>**
    - **F** charge you a penalty fee
    - **G** forgive you, if it is the first time
    - **H** close your account temporarily
    - **J** hold the check until you have enough money in the account

11. **How do banks earn a profit?**
    - **A** They charge customers more to borrow money than they pay to customers who save.
    - **B** They only loan money to individuals and businesses with excellent credit ratings.
    - **C** They transfer funds to overseas banks that pay greater interest.
    - **D** They invest customers' savings in the stock market.

✔ Test-Taking Tip

If more than one choice for a multiple-choice question seems correct, ask yourself if each choice completely answers the question. If a choice is only partially true, it is probably not the correct answer.

Directions: Look at the graphic below. Then answer questions 12 through 15.

12. On December 12, 2014, Clara Partridge needs to write a check to the Leadville Water Co. in the amount of $153.23. What should she write on the line that begins "Pay to the Order Of"?

  F Clara Partridge

  G December 12, 2014

  H Leadville Water Company

  J one hundred fifty and 23/100

13. What information must be added to the back of this check for it to be cashed?

  A the recipient's account number

  B the account holder's signature

  C the account holder's address

  D the recipient's signature

14. If Clara's payment to the Leadville Water Co. is due on the 12th of every month, which of the following could she set up to help ensure that her payment will always be on time?

  F a savings account

  G an account balance

  H an interest payment

  J an electronic transfer

15. Which number on this check designates the specific bank for this checking account?

  A 1000

  B 1936

  C 000000186

  D 000000529

This lesson will help you identify several basic types of consumer credit, compare the different types of consumer credit, and describe situations in which each type of credit is useful. Use it with Core Lesson 8.2 *Types of Consumer Credit* to reinforce and apply your knowledge.

Key Concept	Core Skills & Practices
Different types of credit have different purposes and different advantages and disadvantages.	• Sequence Events • Judge the Relevance of Information

Credit

Credit allows you to buy something you want or need and then pay back the creditor over time.

1. **Secured loan interest rates are usually low because the**
   A lenders have more money
   B lenders assume very little risk
   C loan is for a short period of time
   D borrowers have higher credit ratings

2. **Why is it important to obtain your credit report periodically?**
   F It prevents creditors from seizing property.
   G It sometimes allows you to delay payment of bills.
   H It allows you to determine whether someone is using your identity.
   J It provides valuable information to banks and credit card companies.

3. **A home equity loan is a secured loan that may help reduce your taxes, if**
   A the interest is tax deductible
   B it is used to purchase a car
   C your credit score is high
   D you pay a lot in interest

4. **How do credit card companies benefit when consumers use their credit cards?**
   F by selling their credit cards to consumers
   G by charging consumers interest and fees on their debts
   H by adding a few percentage points to the cost of items sold
   J by charging participating retail outlets 5 percent on each sale

Directions: Look at the chart. Then answer questions 5 through 8.

The following chart shows Mr. Fernandez's credit scores from 2009 to 2012.

Year	Credit Score
2009	560
2010	620
2011	500
2012	540

5. **Which phrase best defines the meaning of the economic term *credit score*?**
   A report by a credit agency of how consistently you pay your bills
   B kind of credit card that allows you to defer payment for a year
   C bonus from banks when you pay your bills on time
   D way of buying something before paying for it

6. **Between 2010 and 2011, Mr. Fernandez most likely**
   F earned more money
   G purchased a new home
   H missed credit card payments
   J obtained a low-interest credit card

7. **In 2012, Mr. Fernandez probably found that**
   A the cost of living was increasing rapidly
   B he had a more difficult time getting credit
   C he no longer had a secure source of income
   D interests rates were lower than they had been

8. **The credit agency that issued Mr. Fernandez's credit scores most likely obtained its information from**
   F employers and retail stores
   G banks and credit card companies
   H the Internal Revenue Service and employers
   J financial institutions and Social Security records

Comparing Types of Credit

Different types of credit have different advantages and disadvantages.

Directions: Read the questions and choose the best answer.

9. **The amount you pay to use credit is the**

   A annual percentage rate

   B finance charge

   C interest rate

   D balance

10. **It is not a good idea to buy a car with a credit card because credit card companies**

    F expect repayment within a short time

    G will report defaults to credit agencies

    H do not lend large amounts of money

    J usually charge high interest rates

11. **An installment loan to buy a home is a good idea, if a person has a down payment and**

    A the buyer has a small source of income

    B they have someone to live with

    C the property value is falling

    D interest rates are low

12. **Legally, you can obtain a free credit report every**

    F year

    G month

    H ten years

    J five years

13. **You can avoid paying any interest on a credit card account by**

    A maintaining a high credit score

    B obtaining a no-interest credit card

    C paying off the card's balance every month

    D keeping a balance of under $100 at all times

14. **Large purchases such as homes or cars are usually obtained using**

    F credit cards

    G secured loans

    H revolving credit

    J unsecured loans

Directions: Read the excerpt. Then answer questions 15 through 18.

A recent study done by two professors at The Ohio State University indicates that younger people are more at risk from credit card debt. For example, a person born between 1980 and 1984 has debt higher than the previous two generations—$5,689 higher than their parents, and $8,156 higher than their grandparents. "Our projections are that the typical credit card holder among younger Americans who keeps a balance will die still in debt to credit card companies."

15. **Total credit card debt in the United States is a detriment to our economic future. Based on the excerpt, this is a serious concern because research shows that**

   A credit card companies will be less likely to lend to younger people

   B the problem seems to be getting more severe with each generation

   C few people are paying down their credit card debt before they die

   D credit card interest continues to rise

16. **Based on the excerpt, one implication of the study is that younger people**

   F buy more than their parents did

   G will not be able to take out loans

   H are making more purchases online

   J are not paying off their balances each month

17. **What can you infer from the passage about the willingness of credit card companies to offer credit to younger people?**

   A Credit card companies want their younger customers to pay off credit card balances each month.

   B Credit card companies see younger people as a good market for more of their products and services.

   C Credit card companies are becoming more strict about the need for potential new customers to have high credit scores.

   D Credit card companies are waiting until potential customers are older to offer their products and services to those customers.

18. **After noting the differences between the debt of people compared to that of their parents and grandparents, how much higher would the next generation's debt be than that of their great-grandparents, assuming the trend remains the same?**

   F $5,689

   G $8,156

   H $10,623

   J $11,378

 Test-Taking Tip

When you read a passage during a test, you need to eliminate information that is not necessary for answering questions. One way to do this is to read the passage, taking notes of important information, and then reviewing the questions to see what information is covered and what is not.

This lesson will help you understand the importance of consumer credit laws, such as the Equal Credit Opportunity Act, the Consumer Credit Protection Act, and the Truth in Lending Act. Use it with Core Lesson 8.3 *Consumer Credit Laws* to reinforce and apply your knowledge.

Key Concept

The federal government enforces laws that provide many safeguards for the consumer using credit.

Core Skills & Practices

- Analyze Point of View
- Identify Author's Bias

Consumer Credit Protections

Since the 1960s, the federal government has passed a variety of consumer credit protection laws to prevent discrimination, to ensure that consumers have clear information about the terms of credit, and to limit fees and interest rates that lenders can charge.

Directions: Read the excerpt. Then answer questions 1 and 2.

If . . . the consumer requests a copy of a consumer report from the person who procured the report, then, within 3 business days of receiving the consumer's request, together with proper identification, the person must send or provide to the consumer a copy of a report and a copy of the consumer's rights as prescribed by the Bureau...

A consumer may elect to have the consumer's name and address excluded from any list provided by a consumer reporting agency under subsection (c)(1)(B) in connection with a credit or insurance transaction that is not initiated by the consumer, by notifying the agency in accordance with paragraph (2).

. . . Except as otherwise provided in this subsection, no person that accepts credit cards or debit cards for the transaction of business shall print more than the last 5 digits of the card number or the expiration date upon any receipt provided to the cardholder at the point of the sale or transaction.

—The Fair Credit Reporting Act

1. **The Fair Credit Reporting Act and its amendments include several provisions, such as**

   A protection from discrimination on the basis of race, sex, or religion

   B allowing consumers access to their credit reports

   C protections against exceeding a credit limit

   D the right to a free credit report each month

2. **The "Opt Out" provision of the Fair Credit Reporting Act says that a consumer may choose to have**

   F his or her name removed from lender marketing lists

   G personal information removed from the credit reporting agency files

   H no credit card business transaction collected by credit reporting agencies

   J his or her name removed from lists shared by a consumer reporting agency

Directions: Read the following questions and choose the best answer.

3. **Which act limits a consumer's *liability*, or legal responsibility, for purchases if a credit card is stolen and used by someone else?**

   A Truth in Lending Act

   B Fair Credit Billing Act

   C Fair Credit Reporting Act

   D Equal Credit Opportunity Act

4. **Which act prohibits discrimination in credit transactions based on race, religion, sex, national origin, age, or marital or economic status?**

   F Truth in Lending Act

   G Fair Credit Billing Act

   H Fair Credit Reporting Act

   J Equal Credit Opportunity Act

5. **Under which act would Congress add additional consumer protection laws that relate to credit?**

   A Truth in Lending Act

   B Fair Credit Billing Act

   C Equal Credit Opportunity Act

   D Consumer Credit Protection Act

Directions: Read the excerpt. Then answer questions 6 and 7.

Dear Editor:

The federal government has tried to protect credit cardholders for years. But problems persist. For example, retailers continue to approve "over the limit" purchases that often result in huge fees from the credit card companies. These companies impose a retroactive interest rate of 25 to 30 percent if a cardholder is one day late! They advertise "No Interest for 6 Months" and then charge huge interest rate if the balance isn't then paid in full. How is a person supposed to get out of debt if penalty rates are 40 percent? We need new legislation to prevent these companies from misleading the public.

Sincerely,
J.Q. Public

6. **The writer believes that which of these has been ineffective?**

   F The Fair Credit and Charge Card Disclosure Act

   G Consumer Financial Protection Bureau

   H The Truth in Lending Act

   J The Credit CARD Act

7. **The writer believes that federal credit card protection has been**

   A inadequate to deal with the problems facing cardholders

   B able to deal with all but a few cardholder problems

   C too tough on credit card companies

   D unenforced since the early 1960s

Recent Credit Protections

The federal government expanded credit protections in the 1980s and 2000s.

Directions: Read the questions and choose the best answer.

8. **Credit card providers are prohibited from offering**

   F rebates

   G insurance

   H no-interest loans

   J frequent-flyer miles

9. **What is the <u>most</u> important thing a prospective credit card owner should know about a credit card?**

   A if there are frequent-flyer miles

   B the over-the-credit-limit fee

   C the cash advance features

   D the APR for purchases

10. **The Consumer Financial Protection Bureau (CFPB) has authority over most federal consumer protection laws and looks out for the interests of which consumers?**

    F those with limited income

    G those who have filed for bankruptcy protection

    H those shopping for financial products or services

    J those shopping for high-value products or services

11. **What event prompted the creation of the Consumer Financial Protection Bureau?**

    A the US financial crisis that began in 2007

    B "the expansion of services offered by credit unions

    C the growth of financial services being offered online

    D the expiration of existing federal consumer protection laws

---

✔ Test-Taking Tip

The more you practice reading different types of texts of different lengths, the better prepared you will be to read and understand passages presented in reading tests. A good way to practice is to read as much as you can about subjects that interest you. Not only will you become a better reader when taking a test, you will also increase your enjoyment of reading.

The Consumer Financial Protection Bureau

The government created the Consumer Financial Protection Bureau to oversee federal consumer protection laws and to look out for the interests of consumers who are shopping for financial products.

Directions: Study the table below and answer questions 12 through 14.

Credit Card Information

New balance	$3,000.00
Minimum payment due	$90.00
Payment due date	4/20/12

Late Payment Warning: If we do not receive your minimum payment by the date listed above, you may have to pay a $35 late fee and your APRs may be increased up to the Penalty APR of 28.99%.

Minimum Payment Warning: If you make only the minimum payment each period, you will pay more in interest and it will take you longer to pay off your balance. For example:

If you make no additional charges using this card and each month you pay...	You will pay off the balance shown on this statement in about...	And you will end up paying an estimated total of...
Only the minimum payment	11 years	$4,745
$103	3 years	$3,712 (Savings = $1,033)

12. **To avoid any interest charges, the consumer should pay**

   F the amount of $1,000.00

   G the balance of $3,000.00

   H the minimum payment of $90.00

   J the suggested payment of $103.00

13. **The notices on this statement reflect a number of changes created by the Consumer Financial Protection Bureau. What caused the creation of this bureau?**

   A irresponsible behavior of all Americans who had loans

   B severe financial crisis in the United States that began in 2007

   C failure of the previous agency concerned with consumer credit laws

   D failure of the Dodd-Frank Wall Street Reform and Consumer Protection Act

14. **This required credit card information was put into place by the**

   F Credit CARD Act

   G Truth in Lending Act

   H Equal Credit Opportunity Act

   J Consumer Credit Protection Act

This lesson will help you understand the development of ancient North Africa and the Indian subcontinent, early Chinese civilization, and ancient Greece and Rome. Use it with Core Lesson 9.1 *Development of Ancient Civilizations* to reinforce and apply your knowledge.

Key Concept

Ancient civilizations shared the same six developments: cities, central government, religion, social and economic classes, art and architecture, and writing.

Core Skills & Practices

- Draw Evidence from Text
- Understand Cause and Effect

Ancient North Africa and the Indian Subcontinent

A civilization is a society in an advanced state of cultural development. Ancient civilizations sprang up in North Africa along the banks of the Nile River and on the Indian subcontinent along the banks of the Indus and Ganges Rivers.

Directions: Study the map. Then answer questions 1 through 4.

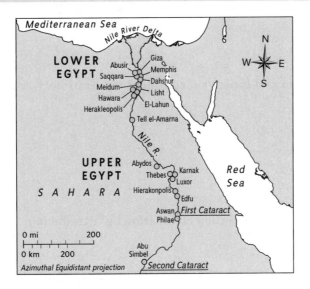

1. **Ancient Egypt is sometimes called the "gift of the Nile," because**
   A the Nile is the world's longest river
   B fishing was one of Egypt's largest industries
   C Egypt depended on the Nile for transportation
   D the Nile's annual floodwaters made agriculture possible

2. **The placement of cities on this map shows how the development of early civilizations depended heavily on**
   F mountains
   G access to water
   H stone architecture
   J religious monuments

3. Egyptians built the pyramids

A near the Nile delta

B to defend against invasion

C on the shores of the Red Sea

D to house government documents

4. The number of pyramids shown on the map reflect the importance Egyptians placed on

F democracy

G mathematics

H philosophy

J religion

Directions: Read the questions and choose the best answer.

5. What did early civilizations on the Indian subcontinent have in common with ancient Egyptian civilization?

A Both had indoor plumbing and running water.

B Both built large religious monuments.

C Both were centered near rivers.

D Both began around 2500 B.C.

6. The economies of the ancient Egyptian and Indian subcontinent civilizations were dependent upon

F agriculture

G hunting

H manufacturing

J trade

7. The Aryans significantly influenced the Indus Valley civilization by introducing

A art

B economics

C farming

D social structure

Early Chinese Civilizations

Like the early civilizations in Egypt and the Indian subcontinent, the first civilization in China began in a river valley. Chinese civilization was based on dynasties, and family was important to the structure of Chinese society.

Directions: Read the excerpt. Then answer questions 8 through 10.

The Mandate of Heaven

To understand almost every aspect of Chinese culture, one must understand the concept of the Mandate of Heaven. It explains the dynastic cycles in China over the centuries beginning around the 11th century B.C.

The Duke of Zhou, younger brother of King Wu of the Western Zhou dynasty, first explained the Mandate of Heaven's four principles: 1. The right to rule is granted by Heaven. 2. There is one Heaven, therefore only one ruler. 3. The right to rule depends on the virtue of the ruler. 4. The right to rule is not limited to one dynasty. In other words, a ruler may lose the Mandate of Heaven. The Zhou dynasty explained its overthrow of the Shang dynasty, based on the Mandate.

8. **As is it used in this passage, the term** *mandate* **most likely means**

   F blessing

   G command

   H favor

   J wish

9. **The Mandate of Heaven was used to explain the overthrow of**

   A Chinese dynasties beginning in the 11th century B.C.

   B Only the Shang dynasty by the Zhou

   D all governments in Asian countries

   C King Wu of the Western Zhou

10. **Based on information in this passage and what you know about ancient Egypt, you can conclude that the ruling dynasties of ancient Egypt and ancient China**

   F thought that life after death was similar to life on Earth

   G believed that their authority came from a divine source

   H presented their rulers as living gods on Earth

   J felt that overthrowing a ruler could be justified

 Test-Taking Tip

Note how much time you are given to complete a test. Keep an eye on the time as you are taking the test. Stop periodically to make sure that you are on target to finish. Plan ahead so you have time at the end of the exam to review your answers. Make sure that you have answered all the questions and have not made any errors.

Ancient Greece and Rome

The ancient civilizations of Greece and Rome were located in the Mediterranean region. Like other ancient civilizations, they also developed in river valleys.

Directions: Read the following questions and choose the best answer.

11. **Which of the following best explains the difference between the governments of ancient Egypt and China and the governments of ancient Greece and Rome?**

    A The governments of Greece and Rome allowed ordinary citizens to participate.

    B The governments of Greece and Rome did not recognize a class system.

    C The governments of Greece and Rome were not based on agriculture.

    D The governments of Greece and Rome had no official rulers.

12. **By the third century B.C, the government of the Roman Republic, like the government of Ancient Athens,**

    F allowed male citizens to participate in government

    G forbade citizens from interfering in economic matters

    H gave citizens the right to veto the actions of the Senate

    J required male citizens to own land to participate in government

13. **Romans established a republic, which is a system of government in which citizens**

    A choose an emperor to govern

    B govern directly through voting

    C elect representatives to govern

    D chosen by one leader make most decisions

14. **How did geography contribute to the rise of the Greek polis?**

    F Greece's resources spurred trade and interaction among groups.

    G Greece's closeness to the Near East influenced the development of the city-state.

    H Rivers created transportation networks that allowed Athens to influence other areas.

    J Geographic barriers separated people, allowing them to develop independent city-states.

15. **The city-state in ancient Greece was usually built at the site of what geographic feature?**

    A hill

    B lake

    C mountain

    D valley

This lesson will help you understand boundaries and borders, why borders often follow natural features, and how cooperation and conflict influence the division of Earth's surface. Use it with Core Lesson 9.2 *Nationhood and Statehood* to reinforce and apply your knowledge.

Key Concept

Political and geographic boundaries divide Earth into different regions and nations.

Core Skills & Practices

- Synthesize Ideas from Multiple Sources
- Analyze Author's Purpose

Boundaries and Borders

Boundaries are lines that separate one area of Earth from another area. Political borders are boundaries separating one state or country from another, creating statehood and nationhood.

Directions: Study the map. Then answer the questions 1 through 3.

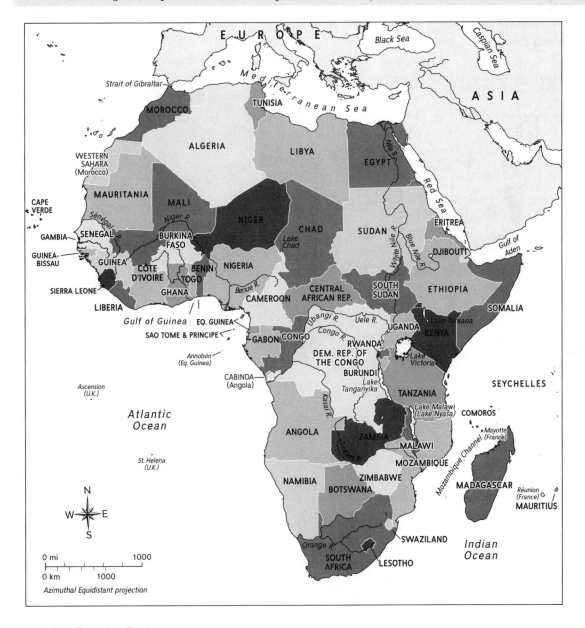

1. **Which two physical boundaries separate Europe and Asia and from Africa?**
   A   Nile River and Mediterranean Sea
   B   Atlantic Ocean and Indian Ocean
   C   Mediterranean Sea and Red Sea
   D   Red Sea and Indian Ocean

2. **How many countries share borders with Mali?**
   F   five
   G   six
   H   seven
   J   eight

3. **The Atlantic Ocean is a physical and political boundary that separates the countries in Africa and Europe from those in**
   A   Antarctica
   B   Asia and Australia
   C   North and South America
   D   North America and East Asia

Directions: Study the map. Then answer questions 4 through 6.

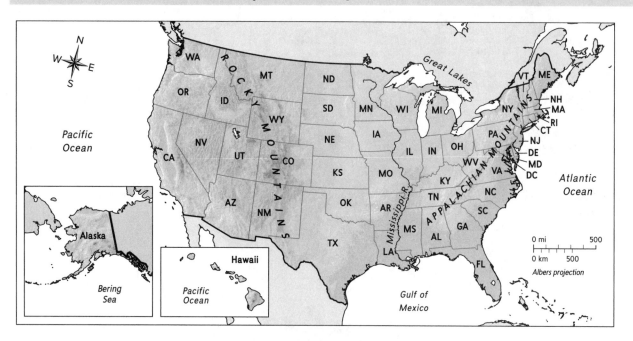

4. **The Mississippi River is a political boundary and a**
   F   parallel
   G   line of longitude
   H   geometric border
   J   physical boundary

5. The Pacific Ocean serves as the border for how many states?

   A three

   B four

   C five

   D six

6. The borders of ten states coincide at the Mississippi River. Which term <u>best</u> fits the meaning of the word *coincide*?

   F blend

   G separate

   H split apart

   J occur together

Geometric Borders

Some borders that follow imaginary lines on Earth—such as lines of longitude and latitude—are called geometric borders.

Directions: Study the map. Then answer questions 7 and 8.

7. The degrees of lines of latitude decrease from

   A north to south

   B south to north

   C east to west

   D west to east

8. Which of these follows a line of longitude?

   F the border between the United States and Canada

   G the southern border of the United States

   H the border between Alaska and Canada

   J the western border of the United States

The Creation of Borders

People create borders that separate ethnic and national groups, sometimes through war and sometimes through negotiations.

Directions: Study the maps. Then answer questions 9 and 10.

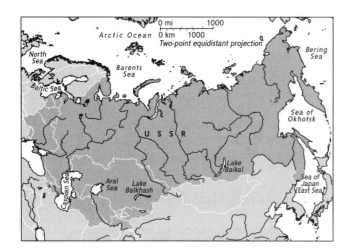

9. The fact that Kazakhstan has separate boundaries in the second map indicates that it has become a(n)

A colony

B isolated region

C physical boundary

D independent nation

10. Because the dissolution of the Soviet Union occurred without a war, these new boundaries were <u>most likely</u> created using

F conflict

G cooperation

H longitude

J negotiation

✔ Test-Taking Tip

When you are taking a test, you might see a detailed image that is associated with a question. When you see something like this on a test, it helps to read the question first to determine exactly what it is asking. Then look at the image with the purpose of gathering only the details that will help you answer the question.

This lesson will help you discuss the effects of population growth and economic development, explain carrying capacity and global warming, define sustainability, and give examples of sustainable development. Use it with Core Lesson 9.3 *Human Activity and the Environment* to reinforce and apply your knowledge.

Key Concept

Economic development and a growing population are affecting the environment on Earth. Many people want to enact new policies to preserve Earth's natural resources.

Core Skills & Practices

• Draw Evidence from Text
• Analyze Ideas

Population Growth and Economic Development

As Earth's population continues to rise, and as more and more of its natural resources are being used, many people are concerned about how these changes will affect our environment.

Directions: Read the passage below. Then answer questions 1 through 3.

Since taking office, I have supported an all-of-the-above energy approach that will allow us to take control of our energy future, one where we safely and responsibly develop America's many energy resources—including natural gas, wind, solar, oil, clean coal, and biofuels—while investing in clean energy and increasing fuel efficiency standards to reduce our dependence on foreign oil.

. . . I have made the largest investment in clean energy and energy efficiency in American history and proposed an ambitious Clean Energy Standard to generate 80 percent of our electricity from clean energy sources like wind, solar, clean coal, and natural gas by 2035.

—President Barack Obama

1. **President Obama's main concern seems to be developing more energy sources that are**
   A expensive
   B nonrenewable
   C profitable
   D renewable

2. **Which of the following best explains why President Obama would take an "all-of-the-above" approach to finding energy sources?**
   F Some citizens refuse to use certain types of energy sources.
   G The president needs to be careful not to alienate any voting group.
   H Without new sources, the United States might exceed its carrying capacity.
   J The United States does not have enough of any one particular source of energy.

3. **By setting a goal of generating 80 percent of electricity from clean energy sources, President Obama is trying to promote**

    A   sustainable development

    B   the greenhouse effect

    C   foreign competition

    D   carrying capacity

Directions: Read the question and choose the best answer.

4. **Which definition below fits the meaning of the word *nonrenewable*?**

    F   not replaceable or not able to be replaced for millions of years

    G   not living within limits with regard to Earth's resources

    H   not having the capacity to be recycled or reused

    J   using up a supply or resource

Global Warming and Climate Change

Carbon dioxide is one of many gases that cause Earth's greenhouse effect, or its ability to prevent some heat from the Sun from escaping back into space. Without the greenhouse effect, Earth would be too cold for life.

Directions: Read the passage below. Then answer questions 5 and 6.

Francisco Estrada is an ecological economist at the Free University in Amsterdam. He studied temperature data from 1850 to 2010 to determine whether there was a correlation between fossil fuel emissions and global warming. Here is some of what he found:

"A cooling period between 1940 and 1970 had previously been chalked up to natural variability and the Sun-shielding effect of pollution emitted by European industries, as they recovered after the Second World War. But Estrada and his colleagues found that it followed a reduction in greenhouse-gas emissions associated with economic downturns, when industries were less active. Significant drops in emissions occurred during the First World War, the Great Depression of the 1930s and the Second World War."

—Hannah Hoag, *Nature*, November 10, 2013

5. **What does Estrada now believe caused the cooling period between 1940 and 1970?**

    A   a decrease in greenhouse gas emissions because industries were less active

    B   an increase in greenhouse gas emissions because of the economic downturn

    C   a decrease in greenhouse gas emissions because of a decrease in the Sun-shielding effect of pollution

    D   an increase in greenhouse gas emissions because of a decrease in the Sun-shielding effect of pollution

6. **Why did greenhouse gas emissions drop during World War I, the Great Depression, and World War II?**

    F   The Sun-shield effect was stronger.

    G   The economy was in an upswing.

    H   Fewer fossil fuels were used.

    J   Industry was less active.

7. **One effect of global climate change is that**

    A water availability is changing

    B the poles are becoming colder

    C water is receding in coastal areas

    D fossil fuels are being completely depleted

8. **Which of the following is a fossil fuel?**

    F carbon dioxide

    G nuclear energy

    H natural gas

    J quartz

Sustainability

Sustainability is a term that refers to living within limits when it comes to the use of natural resources.

Directions: Read the questions and choose the best answer.

9. **One way to support sustainable development would be to**

    A call for higher emissions standards

    B pressure oil companies to avoid oil spills

    C oppose development of hydroelectric power

    D advocate for more public and less private transportation

10. **Automakers will produce smaller, more fuel-efficient automobiles when**

    F people begin using alternative transportation

    G consumer demand for them increases

    H the price of gasoline drops sharply

    J fewer people can afford large cars

11 **In addition to the size and growth of Earth's human population, which of the following is a reason why Earth's natural resources are being depleted?**

    A Decreased access to resources is leading to wasteful consumption.

    B People are destroying resources to protest their unequal distribution.

    C Natural resources are becoming more costly to produce and distribute.

    D Higher standards of living are allowing more people to use more resources.

12 **The production of automobiles with higher fuel efficiency is <u>most</u> dependent on**

    F government regulation

    G government subsidies

    H consumer demand

    J technology

Directions: Study the graph. Then answer questions 13 through 15.

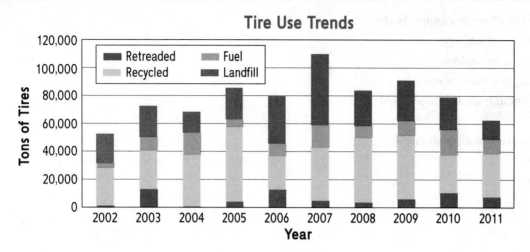

Tire Use Trends

Source: http://www.ecy.wa.gov/programs/swfa/tires/reuse.html

13. How does the graph illustrate the concept of sustainable development?

A It shows how many natural resources are being used to make new tires.

B It shows that retreaded tires are the smallest portion of tires each year.

C It shows that the amount of tires used as fuel has decreased.

D It shows the amount of tires being reused and recycled.

14. Which year shows the <u>most</u> sustainability for tires?

F 2003

G 2005

H 2007

J 2011

15. Which of the following events might cause the number of reused or recycled tires to decline?

A a ban on tires in landfills

B a rise in safety concerns about retreaded tires

C the development of an improved process for turning used tires into fuel

D the adoption of shredded-tire playground surfaces by more school systems

 **Test-Taking Tip**

When you are answering questions about a graph, study the graph first to see any patterns or trends that the graph reveals.

This lesson will help you understand that natural resources are distributed and utilized in various ways, recognize the many ecosystems on Earth, and consider weather and climate systems. Use it with Core Lesson 10.1 *Concepts of Region and Place* to reinforce and apply your knowledge.

Key Concept	**Core Skills & Practices**
Planet Earth is made of many interconnected physical systems, including land, water, plants, animals, and weather.	• Use Maps • Use Graphs

Earth's Structure and Regions

The surface of Earth is composed of vast oceans as well as large landmasses with mountains, hills, valleys, and plains.

Directions: Read the following questions and choose the best answer.

1. **How does a plateau differ from a plain?**
   A A plain is flat, whereas a plateau is hilly.
   B A plain is characterized by trees, whereas a plateau is not.
   C Both occur near water, but a plain connects two larger land areas.
   D Both are flat areas, but a plateau is higher than its surrounding areas.

2 **Flowering plants, shrubs, coyotes, ground-nesting birds, and prairie dogs are found in which ecosystem?**
   F desert
   G forest
   H grassland
   J tundra

3 **What continent is home to only one biome?**
   A Africa
   B Antarctica
   C Australia
   D South America

Directions: Study the image of Earth below. Then answer questions 4 through 6.

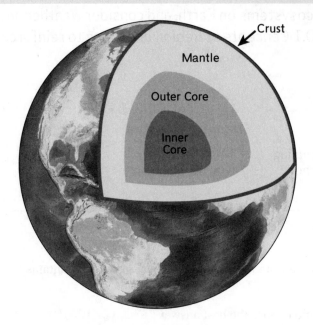

4. **All living organisms on Earth live on the layer known as the**
    F   continent
    G   crust
    H   mantle
    J   ocean

5. **The difference between the inner and outer core can <u>best</u> be described as the difference between**
    A   liquid and solid
    B   land and water
    C   gas and solid
    D   hot and cold

6. **The thickest layer shown in this graphic is made of**
    F   hot gas
    G   solid rock
    H   solid metal
    J   liquid metal

Directions: Study the graph. Then answer questions 7 and 8.

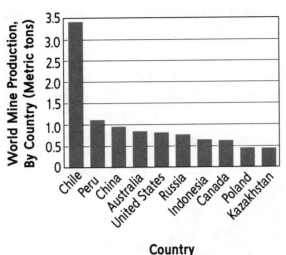

Copper Production
(Thousands of Metric Tonnes)

Source: http://www.indexmundi.com/minerals/?
product=copper&graph=production

7. **Which two continents lead the world in copper production?**

   A Asia and Africa

   B Asia and Europe

   C Australia and Europe

   D North and South America

8. **Chile produces more copper than the**

   F next three highest producers combined

   G next six highest producers combined

   H rest of the world combined

   J world can use at this time

Ecosystems

An ecosystem is a community of organisms in an area and the natural resources with which the community interacts.

Directions: Read the following question. Then select the correct answers.

9. **Which region is <u>more likely</u> to include a tundra ecosystem?**

   A Arctic

   B Amazon jungle

   C Hawaiian Islands

   D Great Lakes region

10. **How does a biome differ from an ecosystem?**

   F   Many similar ecosystems in one region make up a biome.

   G   An ecosystem occurs on land, and a biome occurs in water.

   H   An ecosystem is an area that contains many unrelated biomes.

   J   Ecosystems are defined by climate, but biomes are defined by plant and animals species.

Weather and Climate

Weather changes daily and includes conditions such as air temperature, wind speed and direction, cloud cover, and amount of precipitation. Climate is determined by the weather patterns that an area experiences over a long period of time.

Directions: Study the map. Then answer questions 11 through 13.

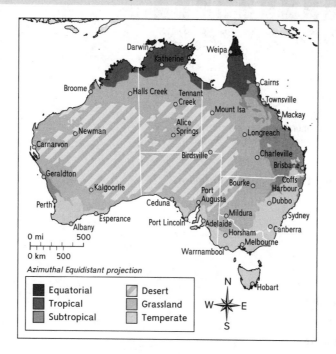

11. **Because Australia is below the Equator, the tropical climate in the country is**

   A   in the North

   B   extremely small

   C   in the Southeast

   D   along the west coast

12. **Australia's large desert climate**

   F   is half the size of the entire country

   G   is more than 1,600 kilometers wide

   H   is next to a subtropical climate

   J   has no human habitation

13. **Which factors <u>most</u> affect the average temperature of an area?**

   A   wind speed and direction, cloud cover, and precipitation

   B   human activity contributing to an increase in carbon dioxide

   C   types of vegetation and variations in soil and other natural resources

   D   elevation, distance from the Equator, distance from a large body of water

This lesson will help you understand the diversity of physical geography and human geography and how landforms affect human settlement. Use it with Core Lesson 10.2 *Natural and Cultural Diversity* to reinforce and apply your knowledge.

Key Concept

Earth is rich in physical and cultural diversity, as seen by its landscapes and its people.

Core Skills & Practices

- Infer
- Evaluate Evidence

Physical Diversity

The landscapes of Earth exhibit vast diversity—from flat plains to rugged mountains and from wetlands and rivers to dry prairies and deserts.

Directions: Read the following questions and choose the best answer.

1. **Which continent is the furthest south?**
   A Africa
   B Antarctica
   C Oceana
   D South America

2. **Earth's five oceans are the Atlantic, Pacific,**
   F Mediterranean, Southern, and Indian
   G Indian, Mediterranean, and Arctic
   H Arctic, Arabian, and Northern
   J Southern, Arctic, and Indian

3. **Climate zones are determined by a region's characteristics such as latitude or distance from the Equator, nearness to a large body of water, air currents and landforms. In which of the following locations might you expect to find an arid, desert-type climate?**
   A northeast coast of China
   B sixty degrees north latitude
   C interior of Australia surrounded by mountains
   D near the Equator and bordered by the Pacific Ocean

4. **Which location is <u>most likely</u> to have the lowest density of plant and animal life?**

   F   Arctic Circle

   G   Central Africa

   H   Southeastern Europe

   J   Northwestern United States

5. **Which definition <u>best</u> fits the meaning of the term *diversity*?**

   A   cultural relevance

   B   ability to adapt

   C   distinctiveness

   D   variety

Cultural Diversity

Just as Earth's physical regions have defining characteristics that set them apart from one another, so do Earth's people have languages, customs, values, and beliefs that define them.

Directions: Read the questions and choose the best answers.

6. **The most commonly spoken language in the world is**

   F   English

   G   German

   H   Mandarin

   J   Spanish

7. **Members of the Indo-European language family include German, French, Italian,**

   A   Japanese, and Mandarin

   B   Sanskrit, and Japanese

   C   Greek, and Sanskrit

   D   Swahili, and Greek

 **Test-Taking Tip**

When you are answering a question related to a chart with a lot of data, read the question first so you can target the specific data in the chart needed to answer the question.

8. **Study the chart.**

Fifteen Largest Ancestries: 2000

In millions, percentage of total population in parentheses.

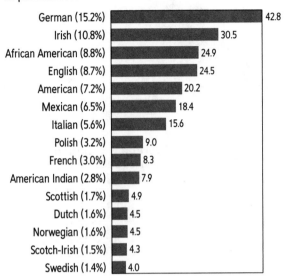

German (15.2%)	42.8
Irish (10.8%)	30.5
African American (8.8%)	24.9
English (8.7%)	24.5
American (7.2%)	20.2
Mexican (6.5%)	18.4
Italian (5.6%)	15.6
Polish (3.2%)	9.0
French (3.0%)	8.3
American Indian (2.8%)	7.9
Scottish (1.7%)	4.9
Dutch (1.6%)	4.5
Norwegian (1.6%)	4.5
Scotch-Irish (1.5%)	4.3
Swedish (1.4%)	4.0

Source: U.S. Census Bureau, Census 2000 special tabulation.

The United States is ethnically diverse. The high number of German, Irish, African American, and English people is largely because

F   more recent immigrants came from these areas

G   people from these regions are immigrating to escape economic conditions

H   war in these regions forced more people to immigrate to the United States

J   these groups came very early and have more descendants than other groups

Landforms and Human Settlement

Physical factors, such as landforms, climate, and environment, affect where people choose to settle and how their culture develops.

Directions: Read the questions and choose the best answer.

9. **The Lakota people lived on the Great Plains of North America. As a consequence, their diet most likely included**

A   bear meat

B   bison

C   fish

D   seagulls

10. **For thousands of years, people in early civilizations chose to settle in**

F   coastal areas

G   mountainous regions

H   rain forests

J   river valleys

Directions: Study the map. Then answer the questions 11 and 12.

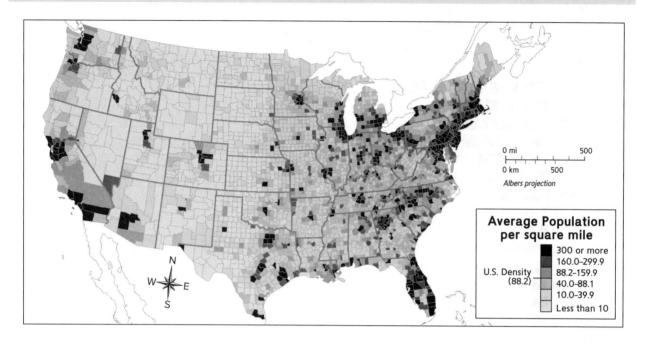

11. The sparse populations of many Western states can be explained by the fact that

A these states were settled last

B these states have fewer natural resources

C most of them have extreme weather conditions

D the government has reserved the land for national parks

12. Based on the map, the large populations of California, Michigan, Ohio, Pennsylvania, Florida, and New York are chiefly explained by the observation that

F people generally prefer to live near large bodies of water

G immigrants are unevenly distributed across the country

H these states have more natural resources

J the climate of these states is temperate

This lesson will help you understand what is meant by the study of demography; recognize that population growth, migrations, and settlement patterns tell a great deal about how humans interact with their environment; and explain the general trend toward urban growth in the United States. Use it with Core Lesson 10.3 *Population Trend and Issues* to reinforce and apply your knowledge.

Key Concept

Humans interact with Earth by moving from place to place, building new communities, and expanding their populations.

Core Skills & Practices

• Analyze Information
• Display Data

Demography

The statistical study of the size, growth, movement, and distribution of people is called demography. Governments and other institutions rely on demographic information to forecast and plan the future.

Directions: Look at the map. Then answer questions 1 and 2.

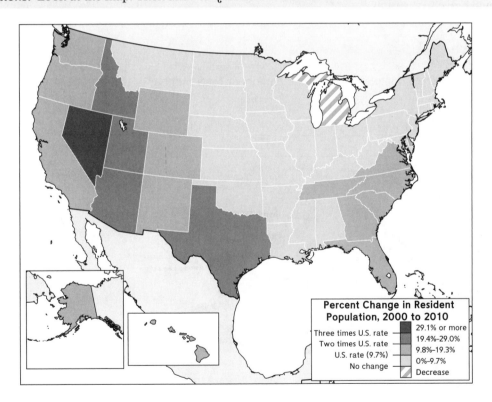

Percent Change in Resident Population, 2000 to 2010

Three times U.S. rate — 29.1% or more
Two times U.S. rate — 19.4%–29.0%
U.S. rate (9.7%) — 9.8%–19.3%
— 0%–9.7%
No change —
Decrease

1. **According to the information given in this graphic, new government services might be needed in the**

    A north central

    B northeast

    C southeast

    D southwest

2. **Which state in the East needed the greatest additional infrastructure (roads, water systems, electricity, etc.) beginning in 1990?**

F Florida

G Georgia

H New York

J North Carolina

Directions: Read the questions and choose the best answer.

3. **Which situation <u>best</u> indicates a growing population?**

A high fertility and high mortality rates

B high fertility and low mortality rates

C low fertility and high mortality rates

D low fertility and low mortality rates

4. **The main reason the government uses census data is to determine**

F which states are the most successful

G where new services might be needed

H how much each person should be taxed

J where citizens should move in the future

Migration and Population

Migration, the movement of people from one place to another, can occur for a number of different reasons.

Directions: Look at the map of migration patterns. Then answer questions 5 through 7.

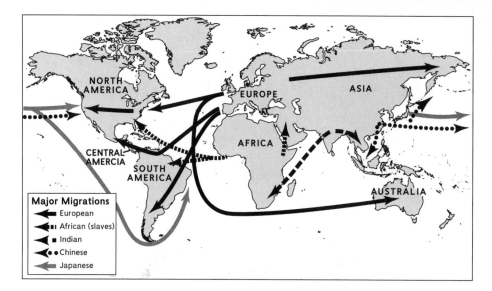

5. **As shown on the map, <u>most</u> people who emigrated from Japan migrated to**

   A North America and South America

   B Europe and South Africa

   C Australia and East Asia

   D Africa and South Asia

6. **Wars, religious and political persecution, and food shortages caused the large migrations of which people beginning in the 17th century?**

   F Africans

   G Asians

   H Chinese

   J Europeans

7. **In the late twentieth century, due to persecution and poor economic conditions, about 12 million people move to the United States from**

   A Rwanda and Burundi

   B Mexico and Asia

   C South Africa

   D Germany

Urban Growth

The last two centuries witnessed a trend toward the movement of people from rural, agricultural areas to urban areas, or cities. More recently, people have been moving from the cities to the suburbs.

Directions: Study the map. Then answer the questions 8 and 9.

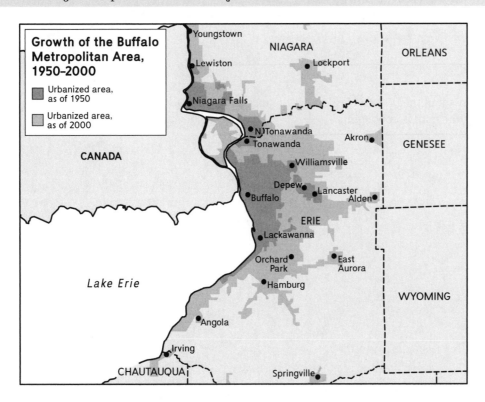

8. **Which two counties have experienced significant population growth?**

   F Erie and Niagara

   G Ontario and Wyoming

   H Chautauqua and Orleans

   J Lancaster and Orchard Park

9. **Buffalo, New York, may fit the description of *urban sprawl* because**

   A more people today live near the center of the city

   B many farmers have moved from Niagara County to the city limits

   C the city population declined, but the metropolitan area has expanded

   D the city continues to incorporate smaller towns into its governed area

Directions: Read the questions and choose the best answer.

10. **Based on what you know about urban migration, which period of population movement is <u>most</u> characterized by *urban sprawl*?**

    F 1800–1850

    G 1870–1950

    H 1950–1980

    J 1980–2010

11. **Based on what you know about urban migration, which period of population movement included the movement of city dwellers to the suburbs just outside the cities?**

    A 1800–1850

    B 1870–1950

    C 1950–1980

    D 1980–2010

 Test-Taking Tip

You can understand a map by reading the title and looking at the map key to determine the information that the map is conveying.

Lesson 1.1

Types of Modern and Historical Governments, p. 1

1. **C** In an oligarchy, all power is held by only a few people.

2. **G** Both the United States Congress and the Canadian Parliament are made up of representatives who are elected by the citizens of their respective countries.

3. **A** A constitutional monarch has mostly ceremonial powers, but a dictator wields absolute power.

4. **F** An autocracy is best described as a government in which the power is held by one person.

5. **D** Both Aristotle and Tocqueville are concerned that people have equal power, regardless of their financial means.

6. **G** Aristotle believed that when government was in the hands of the rich, whether they were many or few, that government was an oligarchy.

7. **D** Tocqueville was concerned that democracy would respect the rights of both capitalists and citizens.

8. **H** Aristotle believes restrictions on the freedom of the poor will be continually disputed.

9. **C** Both documents state that government is instituted to safeguard the rights of the people and that just power is derived from the consent of the people.

10. **H** The Bill of Rights was added to the United States Constitution to protect individual liberties, such as freedom of speech, freedom of assembly, and the right to a speedy and public trial.

11. **A** The Fifteenth Amendment extends the right to vote to African American men, but women, regardless of race, were only allowed to vote upon passage of the Nineteenth Amendment.

12. **H** The Twenty-Sixth Amendment set the voting age for state and federal elections at eighteen.

13. **D** The Twenty-Fourth Amendment made unconstitutional the practice of requiring voters to pay a poll tax before they could vote.

14. **F** A democracy is a form of government in which the people, or the governed, rule.

15. **B** The purpose of both the Bill of Rights and the Magna Carta was to protect individual rights and limit the power of government.

16. **J** The amendment process was included because the authors of the Constitution knew it would need to change with the times in order to stay relevant.

Lesson 1.2

American Constitutional Democracy, p. 5

1. **D** The Framers of the Articles of Confederation feared that a strong central government would become too powerful.

2. **H** A government based on a constitution holds only those powers granted in its constitution.

3. **C** Courts and tax collectors seized farms as repayment of debt and taxes, leading farmers to attack courts and to raid state arsenals for weapons

4. **G** Citizens hold the power in a government by electing their own representatives at all levels of government.

5. **A** The executive branch exercises checks and balances on the legislative and judicial branches by holding the power to nominate federal judges.

6. **H** By creating three branches of government with separate roles and responsibilities, the people had less fear of being too strictly governed by a leader or small group of leaders.

7. B Federalism is the process by which powers and responsibilities are shared by local, state, and central elements of a government.

8. J A faction is a smaller group of people who hold different views, which they make clear to the larger group.

9. A Madison believed that freedom (liberty) would not need to be limited, because the freedom exercised by many other groups would be enough to keep a faction from taking control.

10. F The rule of law means that the law is preeminent over any other factor, including any leader, group, or concern.

11. C The colonists wanted to be sure that the rights that were violated by the British before and during the war—freedom of speech and the press, the right to bear arms, the right against illegal searches and seizures, for example—would be addressed in the new constitution.

12. J Forty-nine percent of those polled were in favor of passing stronger gun laws, while fifty percent were opposed, indicating that Americans are evenly divided on the issue of stronger gun laws.

13. A An amendment must be proposed by Congress and then ratified by a three-fourths majority of the states.

14. H New amendments to the Constitution ensure that it is connected to current issues as they occur.

Lesson 1.3

Structure of American Government, p. 9

1. C The president's chief job is to run the executive department.

2. F The first statement of the Presidential Oath of Office—"that I will faithfully execute the Office of President"—defines his primary responsibility.

3. C The checks and balances written into the Constitution, which allow each branch of government (executive, legislative, judicial) to "check" or prevent the others from becoming too powerful, includes the power of Congress to amend a law found unconstitutional by the Supreme Court.

4. H The president and Congress share military powers.

5. A The president can use television, radio, and the Internet to appeal directly to the public, going over the heads of Congress to make his case.

6. J The author implies that less media reach and a different notion of the role of the president meant that before the 20th century, presidents did not have as much influence on the legislative process.

7. B The power of both the federal and state governments to establish banks is a concurrent power.

8. J By allowing the states to tax the federal government, the states could use that power to weaken federal banks and other services, giving states unintended power to control certain aspects of the federal government.

9. C The judicial branch originally was supposed to hear cases only involving leaders of other nations or between states in the United States.

10. H A referendum is the power to overturn legislation passed by a legislature or by voters by submitting that legislation to a popular vote.

11. B Both Congress and state legislatures have the power to borrow money.

12. G The lieutenant governor, like the vice president, presides over the legislature and replaces the governor if he dies, resigns, or is removed from office.

13. D The power to levy taxes, hold elections, and borrow money belongs to both the state and federal governments, but the power to establish schools belongs only to the state governments

Lesson 2.1

Individual Rights and Responsibilities, p. 13

1. **C** The right to be free from discrimination at work is a civil right.

2. **G** Mason's ideas regarding due process were expressed in the Sixth Amendment.

3. **C** The Establishment Clause prevents the government from establishing or supporting any religion.

4. **G** The right against self-incrimination described in this ruling is protected by the Fifth Amendment.

5. **A** Poll taxes and literacy tests were obstacles set up to prevent African Americans from voting

6. **J** In 1896 the Supreme Court ruled that segregation was legal under the "separate but equal" doctrine.

7. **B** Dr. King's views are most clearly reflected in the Supreme Court's decision in *Brown* v. *Board of Education, Topeka, Kansas,* which declared segregation in public facilities unconstitutional.

8. **F** Suffrage is the right to vote in a political election.

9. **A** During and after World War II, working women found that they were not paid the same as men, were not able to get the same kinds of jobs as men, and were often given jobs that did not allow them to advance.

10. **H** The Equal Pay Act of 1963, which made it illegal to pay men more than women for the same job, was passed after women gained the right to vote in national elections, but before it was illegal to discriminate against women in hiring.

Lesson 2.2

Political Parties, Campaigns, and Elections, p. 17

1. **B** By identifying issues and concerns that were shared by different types of Americans, Sen. Obama was most likely trying to appeal to independent voters.

2. **H** Senator Obama's speech helped outline his party's beliefs, a task that is one of a national convention's main goals.

3. **C** Third-party candidates often deal with an issue or a set of issues that some voters believe the major parties are not adequately addressing.

4. **G** Roosevelt's candidacy likely split the votes that the Republican candidate would have received, leaving the Democratic candidate with the highest number of votes.

5. **A** The nature of the two-party system means that the Democratic and Republican parties wield more power and have more money, both of which influence the outcome of elections.

6. **H** In American political cartoons, the elephant symbolizes the Republican party, so Roosevelt pushing an elephant with a load bearing the words *Panama Canal Project* symbolizes the president's push to convince Republicans to back that project.

7. **B** The electoral vote, which determines the outcome of presidential elections, is determined by electors of each state, whereas the popular vote is the total number of votes cast for a presidential candidate.

8. **H** George W. Bush had won the most electoral votes. This won him the presidency, even though he lost the popular vote.

9. **B** A lobbyist works for an interest group in swaying public officials toward policies that benefit the interest group.

10. **J** Because they charge high fees for their services, lobbyists give wealthy individuals and groups more influence over the legislative process.

Lesson 2.3

Structure of American Government, p. 21

1. **C** As it is used in this context, "domestic" refers to things that happen within one's own country.

2. **H** *Posterity* refers to future generations.

3. **C** The federal government handles policy issues related to selective service.

4. **H** The purpose of federal government policies is to set out laws and guidelines that address problems and issues that affect everyone in the nation.

5. **B** Each city or town is responsible for determining sanitation and waste collection standards.

6. **F** While weight limits falls under transportation policy, emissions falls under environment policy, and medical liability coverage falls under healthcare policy, the seatbelt requirement is a public safety policy.

7. **C** Once Congress passes a new policy or the president signs an order for a new policy, it is up to government agencies to implement the policy.

8. **F** The rules of a public institution would be public policy.

9. **D** Since the final step in the public policy process involves evaluating the effectiveness of the policy, public policy is always in the process of being reshaped and refined.

10. **J** The next step in the process after implementation of a policy is the evaluation of the results.

11. **B** Interest groups normally contribute to the process of policy formation.

12. **H** Special interest groups are organized around specific issues, like preventing texting while driving, while public interest groups work for changes in public policy, and economic interest groups focus on business policy.

13. **C** Special interest groups are devoted to addressing a specific concern or issue.

14. **G** Lobbying is a process by which individuals and interest groups can influence the lawmaking process.

15. **D** According to this ruling, direct personal contact, such as buying lunch or dinner for government officials, can threaten the democratic process.

16. **H** Citizens can indirectly influence public policy by exerting pressure on Congress.

Lesson 3.1

American Revolution, p. 25

1. **D** The Mayflower Compact was a written agreement that set out the rules by which the Pilgrims would govern themselves.

2. **H** Pennsylvania was settled by those seeking religious freedom.

3. **B** This document is an example of a constitution, or a written code of rules.

4. **G** A colony is a land controlled by another nation.

5. **A** Dickinson, like many colonists, opposed the Townshend Acts because they levied taxes on the colonists, who were not represented in the British Parliament.

6. **J** Many colonists responded to these taxes by refusing to buy the taxed goods.

7. **B** As a result of the Boston Tea Party, parliament passed the Coercive Acts to punish Boston.

8. **H** Since this passage asks the king to maintain peace and help his subject—that is, the colonists—we can conclude that it is taken from the Olive Branch Petition.

9. **B** The Olive Branch Petition was an attempt at a truce following the Battles of Lexington and Concord.

10. **F** The king rejected the Olive Branch Petition.

11. **D** The central idea of this passage is that the war nearly doubled Britain's debt. This debt led to the monetary concerns of the colonists.

12. **F** This sentence states the problem that the British faced after the war—the cause. It also states the new policy that was the response to that problem—the effect.

13. **D** The government created by the Articles of Confederation was too weak and did not have the power to tax and pay off debts incurred by the Revolutionary War

14. **H** The Articles of Confederation provided for a unicameral legislature, whereas the Constitution provides for a bicameral legislature: the Senate and the House of Representatives

15. **D** The Great Compromise made population the basis of representation in the House, but each state had an equal vote in the Senate.

Lesson 3.2

A New Nation, p. 29

1. **D** The Northwest Ordinance of 1787 established the process by which new states could be added to the Union.

2. **F** A territory is defined as an area of land that is controlled by a government.

3. **C** The Land Ordinance of 1785 made land available for $1.00 per acre, attracting thousands of settlers and leading to the admission of five states.

4. **H** All of these offices were originally appointed by President Washington.

5. **B** In 1794, Tecumseh, a Shawnee leader, tried to unite other tribes against white settlers in the Ohio Valley in the Battle of Fallen Timbers

6. **F** As a strict constructionist, Jefferson would not have proceeded with any activity that was not specifically given to him in the Constitution.

7. **C** Jefferson pushed past his own concerns in order to provide for a growing nation, both in land and natural resources.

8. **F** In December 1814, two weeks before the Battle of New Orleans, the Treaty of Ghent was signed, ending the war.

9. **B** In the buildup to the War of 1812, Britain seized ships carrying wheat and cotton, directly affecting Southern and Western economies, and this situation increased tensions between Western settlers and American Indians.

10. **H** One of the positive outcomes of winning the War of 1812 was a strong feeling of American nationalism.

11. **B** The concept of Manifest Destiny drove the United States to acquire new territories; the United States annexed Texas in 1848.

12. **J** Manifest Destiny was the belief that Americans were destined to settle all of North America from the Atlantic Ocean to the Pacific Ocean.

13. **C** Under the justification of Manifest Destiny, American settlers pressured the United States government to take over Native American lands.

Lesson 3.3

Civil War and Reconstruction, p. 33

1. **D** The trade route followed by many trading ships was shaped like a triangle and became known as triangular trade.

2. **H** Since the plantation system relied on slave labor, wealthy planters would be most likely to support the expansion of slavery.

3. **C** Abolitionists opposed slavery.

4. **A** Rum was shipped from the colonies to Africa. Answers A, B, and D traveled along the other legs of the route.

5. **C** Since each state is represented by two Senators, the addition of a new slave state would upset the balance between free and slave states in the Senate.

6. **G** To preserve the balance between slave and free states in the Senate, Maine was admitted to the Union at the same time as Missouri.

7. **D** The Missouri Compromise closed the area known as Unorganized Territory to slavery.

8. **J** When Lincoln gave his address, there were still some slave states that stayed in the Union, and Lincoln did not want to alienate them by attacking the slave states that had seceded.

9. **D** Lincoln used persuasive language to try to convince the Confederate states to re-join the Union.

10. **G** The Confederate attack on Fort Sumter signaled the beginning of the Civil War.

11. **A** Because many of the battles were fought in the South, the South had a familiarity with battlegrounds that the North did not have.

12. **H** By having ex-Confederates swear loyalty to the Union, Johnson hoped to prevent them from declaring war on the Union again

13. **A** By the 1870's, economic concerns had caused many Northerners to abandon the cause of Reconstruction.

14. **J** Southern governments instituted black codes to limit the rights of African Americans following the Civil War.

15. **A** The Thirteenth Amendment abolished slavery in the United States.

Lesson 3.4

European Settlement and Population of the Americas, p. 37

1. **C** Northern Europe, with more than 7,876,000 immigrants, was the source of the largest group of immigrants.

2. **G** Because of the large influx of Southern and Eastern Europeans during this period, cities in the northeast became overcrowded.

3. **D** Most Latin American immigrants during this period worked as farmers in the southwestern United States.

4. **F** Democracy in the United States was a pull factor; the other choices are push factors.

5. **D** Since it describes cramped, unsanitary conditions, this passage is most likely about life in a tenement house.

6. **G** In crowded tenement houses, poor sanitation often led to outbreaks of disease.

7. **C** The poor working class most likely lived in tenements in city neighborhoods near factories, railroad yards, and slaughterhouses.

8. **G** People moved from the farm to the city because of the pull factor of available jobs; push factors included falling farm prices and a lower need for farm workers.

9. **B** Nativists were native-born American citizens who were fearful of increased immigration.

10. **H** Immigrants from southern and eastern Europe had religious and cultural traditions that differed from those of many native-born Americans.

11. **B** The Chinese Exclusion Act of 1882 placed extreme limits on the number of Asians who could enter the United States.

12. **H** Prior to 1915 (1914), war in Europe caused a dramatic drop in immigration from that region.

Lesson 4.1

World War I, p. 41

1. **C** The value of concern for lives and property after the sinking of the battleship *Maine* was the deciding factor in the United States' decision to enter the war.

2. **F** By specifying that the United States was not acting to secure an empire, Congress was trying to prove that imperialism was not one of its motives.

3. **D** To support its new position in the world, the United States increased the size and strength of its navy.

4. **G** Because Serbia was closely allied with Russia, when Austria-Hungary declared war on Serbia, Russia and its allies entered the conflict.

5. **A** This alliance, or group of countries joined together by a common cause, became known as the Central Powers.

6. **G** Because it offers Mexico support if it declared war on the United States, this passage is most likely taken from the Zimmerman Telegram, which was written by a German foreign minister.

7. **A** The United States had longstanding ties to France and Great Britain, but many German and Irish Americans favored the Central Powers.

8. **J** Germany's policy of unrestricted submarine warfare, coupled with the release of the Zimmermann Telegram, caused Congress to declare war on Germany.

9. **B** Until Russia withdrew from the war in 1918, Germany was forced to fight a war on two different fronts.

10. **H** Wilson was a supporter of the League of Nations. Because the address expresses his wish that "the world be made fit and safe to live in," it reflects this support.

11. **D** Many senators feared that membership in the League of Nations would cause the United States to lose its sovereignty, or ability to act on its own, in case of war.

12. **F** Eastern Europe was drastically changed because of territory taken from Germany, Russia, and Austria-Hungary to form new nations.

Lesson 4.2

World War II, p. 45

1. **B** After being made chancellor, Hitler suspended the constitution, and therefore did not need the approval of the legislature to act.

2. **J** Totalitarian governments attempt to control every aspect of society, including politics, economics, and culture.

3. **A** Referring to the conditions of the Treaty of Versailles as "shackles" is an example of bias because it shows only one side of an issue.

4. **J** One of the ways Hitler built his support among the German people was to promise to stop the payment of reparations.

5. **D** In 1941, Hitler added the nations of the Balkans to his growing empire.

6. **H** Since he is referring to a embarking on a "Great Crusade" in 1944, we can conclude that Eisenhower is speaking before D-Day, the invasion of France.

7. **A** FDR's list of Japanese actions before using that phrase shows that he wants to describe Japanese aggression.

8. **J** FDR wanted people to know that Japan caused the war by its "unprovoked and dastardly attack" on Pearl Harbor.

9. **C** The United States demanded their unconditional surrender as the only acceptable end to the war with Japan, even at the cost of dropping atomic bombs on their country.

10. **J** The Holocaust was a result of a specific policy, "the final solution," planned by German leaders and carried out by thousands of people who were part of the genocide.

11. **B** First the bombing of Hiroshima, then Nagasaki, with atomic weapons was the result of Japan's refusal to surrender offered by the Allies in the summer of 1945.

12. **G** This order, which in effect classified the West Coast as a war zone, was targeted mainly at Japanese Americans.

Lesson 4.3

The Cold War, p. 49

1. **D** After the war, Germany was divided into four zones, each occupied by one of the Allied nations. The zone occupied by the Soviet Union became communist and was ideologically separated from the western areas.

2. **J** Turkey shared a border with the Soviet Union.

3. **D** The waterways into West Germany from the North Sea were important for shipping goods into West Germany, and having Denmark aligned with the US and Great Britain meant those lanes would remain open.

4. **G** The one area of agreement among the leaders was the creation of the UN to negotiate disputes among nations.

5. **B** Under a policy of containment, the United States sought to slow the expansion of the Soviet Union's influence, rather than face the Soviet Union in open conflict.

6. **F** Under the Marshall Plan, the United States provided "guidance" and security to the nations of western Europe in the form of economic aid.

7. **A** The North Atlantic Treaty Organization was created to stop Soviet expansion in Europe.

8. **G** President Truman then launched the Berlin Airlift. For ten months, American and British planes airlifted millions of tons of supplies to West Berliners.

9. **C** Kennedy sent more troops to West Berlin and called army reserve units to active duty.

10. **G** Winston Churchill gave this border its nickname, the "Iron Curtain."

11. **D** The United States and the Soviets were rarely in agreement about important international conflicts and issues, and each had a veto in the Security Council.

12. **J** Following the communist takeover of Cuba in 1959, thousands of refugees fled to the United States.

13. **B** Kennedy's refusal to provide air support for the Bay of Pigs invasion contributed to the failure of the United States-backed rebellion in Cuba.

14. **H** President Johnson tried to stop the spread of communism in Southeast Asia by sending troops to South Vietnam.

Lesson 4.4

Societal Changes, p. 53

1. **A** According to the speech, the Great Society is "a place where man can renew contact with nature."

2. **H** According to the speech, the Great Society "demands an end to poverty and racial injustice."

3. **B** The EEOC, Equal Employment Opportunity Commission, was set up by the Civil Rights Act to investigate charges of discrimination in the workplace.

4. **F** VISTA helped poor people improve their lives in those places.

5. **C** Only the initial break-in appears to have occurred, as Nixon feels free to turn his attention to other matters instead of defending himself.

6. **J** The Watergate scandal led to the resignation of Richard Nixon, thus it was the biggest challenge of his presidency.

7. **D** The Paris Peace Accord, which ended the Vietnam War ended in 1973, was reached during the presidency of Richard Nixon.

8. **G** Nixon states that United States and Soviet negotiators are meeting to limit nuclear arms and reduce the threat of nuclear war.

9. **B** SALT was an agreement to freeze the production of long-range offensive missiles.

10. **H** Reforms by Gorbachev that had the goal of greater openness in the Soviet Union led to its eventual dissolution.

11. **D** China and the Soviet Union had several conflicts, both military and diplomatic, during the Cold War as they fought for worldwide influence.

12. **G** Nixon's visit to China ended 25 years of diplomatic silence between the United States and China.

13. **C** In 1971, Nixon adopted the policy of détente, which was meant to relax tensions between countries.

Lesson 4.5

Foreign Policy in the 21st Century, p. 57

1. **B** Osama bin Laden attempted to force Westerners from the Middle East when US troops were stationed in Saudi Arabia.

2. **J** The bombing of the USS Cole occurred the year before the attacks of the World Trade Center and Pentagon.

3. **A** The al-Qaeda group supports the establishment of theocracies in Islamic nations.

4. **H** Following the attacks on the World Trade Center and Pentagon, the United States led a coalition force that overthrew the Taliban government in Afghanistan.

5. **D** Bush states that the attacks were against the American way of life and its freedom and opportunity.

6. **G** Terrorism is a political strategy that uses violence against people or property to achieve a goal.

7. D President Bush's first response to the attacks of September 11, 2001 was to launch a war against Afghanistan.

8. J This timeline shows how the terrorist attacks affected US foreign policy.

9. C The UN did not support the invasion of Iraq.

10. F Since he identifies hostile actions committed by the Iraqi government, it is most likely that President Bush was arguing in favor of invading Iraq.

11. B Sentence 5 uses imagery of mothers and their dead children to evoke an emotional response.

12. J The claim that Iraq has "something to hide" is vague and cannot be fact-checked.

13. C President Bush viewed these nations as an "axis of evil" because each nation was developing weapons of mass destruction that could be used against the United States.

Lesson 5.1

Markets, Competition, and Monopolies, p. 61

1. B A market is an arrangement or relationship that makes it easier to buy and sell, that is exchange goods and services.

2. H A market is also a place where goods and services are exchanged. This occurs at a golf course with members paying for the opportunity to play golf or to take golf lessons. Goods and services are not exchanged in a forest preserve, a classroom, or an aircraft carrier.

3. B The invention of money made trading easier once specialized tasks were developed in complex civilizations in which barter no longer worked.

4. G Price is determined by both how much buyers want an item and how much money the seller is willing to accept in trade, regardless of the costs of production.

5. C When resources are scarce or demand for goods and services are high, those without money are at a disadvantage in a market economy.

6. F Auto repair shops offer both services—fixing cars—and goods (parts, tires).

7. D Economic systems answer three questions: what goods and services to produce, how to produce them, and for whom to produce them.

8. H The price of goods and services forces buyers to make choices, which determines distribution.

9. C The ad shows services the restaurant provides that sets it apart from the competition.

10. G Self-interest is the motivation for every transaction, not benevolence.

11. A Smith says that both the buyer and seller serve their own self-interest. When each is satisfied with the bargain, the transaction is made.

12. F One of the chief characteristics of a monopoly is that it produces a unique product, one for which there is no easy substitute.

13. D Patent law allows a technological monopoly to have the exclusive right to use and profit from the technology it spent money to research and develop.

14. G The government passes antitrust laws to keep markets competitive and provide freedom of choice for the consumer.

15. B Both laws were intended to prevent new monopolies from forming and break up those that already exist.

Lesson 5.2

Factors of Production, p. 65

1. **C**   Scarcity is the combination of a product's having value and its being in shorter supply than the number of people who want to own it.

2. **G**   When the quantity of a product is greater than the demand for it, the price usually goes down.

3. **A**   You gave up dinner at the restaurant in exchange for the better phone, so that was what it "cost" you to make that decision.

4. **G**   Business owners can conserve natural resources but cannot control their availability.

5. **B**   Entrepreneurship involves beginning a new business and using creativity to introduce new production methods.

6. **G**   The main factor Samuel Colt changed was how he directed his employees' work processes, making their work more efficient.

7. **C**   By focusing on one or two repeated skills, each worker could perfect and become faster at that skill, and the combined effort would result in a better revolver made in less time.

8. **G**   The improved speed and efficiency would allow the business to make more products with a smaller labor force.

9. **B**   The channel wrapper is a piece of equipment used to produce a good, so it is a capital resource.

10. **J**   The addition of the channel wrapper reduced the most labor-intensive part of the process of producing candy.

11. **C**   If the raw materials needed to create a product are unavailable or in short supply, the manufacturer may find a replacement material in order to continue production.

12. **H**   When an industry has dominated a region for more than a generation, the workforce tends to develop and support those skills needed for that industry rather than developing, valuing, and supporting other skills needed for industries not found in that region.

13. **D**   Texas is within the highest rate of entrepreneurship shown on the map, 0.354% to 0.534%.

Lesson 5.3

Profits and Productivity, p. 69

1. **D**   2009 marks the lowest point on the graph, when companies began building between 400,000 and 800,000 units.

2. **F**   It is better to begin a business during a period when your main product or service is increasingly in demand.

3. **D**   People were buying more homes, which means there would be a market for your business. 1995 was not the peak of demand.

4. **F**   Profit is money earned after expenses are paid.

5. **B**   Entrepreneurs take risks to make a profit, but they try to lessen those risks by keeping expenses low.

6. **H**   A temporary drop in production would be the opportunity cost associated with training workers, investing in research, and purchasing new equipment.

7. **B**   Research and development could occur without impact on existing production.

8. **J**   Pharmaceutical companies spend more, overall, than the other company types.

9. **B**   Spending money on research and development can make profits for companies.

10. F These are capital resources and are used to produce other goods.

11. B The factors of production—human resources, natural resources, capital resources, and entrepreneurship—cannot be bought or sold in a traditional economy.

12. J The United States government cannot take away a citizen's private property without proper compensation.

13. D Traditional economies change little from generation to generation, so they are only found in the most remote regions.

14. H Workers who receive economic rewards for their labor often work hard to win those incentives, especially if they have been deprived of them previously.

Lesson 5.4

Specialization and Comparative Advantage, p. 73

1. C Farmers in Idaho can produce potatoes using fewer resources than farmers in other states.

2. F To be efficient, farmers must be able to produce desired results without wasting material, time, or energy.

3. C An absolute advantage means that a company can produce a product using fewer resources than other companies.

4. J Today, Americans specialize by working in one type of career field. They do not tan their own leather; they buy it from someone else who does that.

5. C Because Company A can make more mops and brooms than Company B, it has a higher absolute advantage.

6. J Those with the lower opportunity cost should specialize in that product or service even if they do not have an absolute advantage.

7. A Look at 0 butter on the x-axis and find where the curve intersects the y-axis. This is at 50 guns.

8. H Look at each data point on the curve and follow it down to the x-axis to find out how much butter can be produced. Then following it left to the y-axis to see how many guns can be produced. Add both numbers together. The highest combination of guns and butter is greater than 70 (40 of butter plus a little more than 30 of guns).

9. A The production possibility frontier for gun production is 50.

10. G Add the maximum number of guns produced on the y-axis to the maximum amount of butter produced on the x-axis (50 guns + 60 butter).

11. D Interdependence happens when producers rely on one another for information, resources, goods, and services.

12. J Because a company can concentrate its resources on one specialized trade, it can increase its productivity.

13. B Interdependence goes hand in hand with specialization, and therefore raises productivity.

14. J The car manufacturer would have difficulty obtaining tires if the rubber industry workers were to strike since rubber is needed to make tires.

Lesson 6.1

Microeconomics, p. 77

1. **D** Producers or sellers influence the supply side of the market.

2. **H** There is government regulation in a mixed economy, but the forces of supply and demand have strong influence in the market.

3. **D** Sellers set the starting price, but consumer demand can influence this price.

4. **G** A rise in prices is most likely due to increased consumer buying.

5. **D** The quantity of CDs sold when the price changed from $10.00 to $5.00 is three, which is a larger amount than any other price change.

6. **F** Look at the y-axis and draw a line to the curve. Then draw a line from that point to the x-axis. This point on the x-axis is the quantity of CDs sold at $15.00.

7. **D** In a demand curve, there is a negative relationship between price and quantity—as one increases, the other decreases.

8. **J** The trend, or direction of change, shown by this graph is that the price of televisions is decreasing over time.

9. **C** The profit motive means the relationship between the price of a good or service and the quantity supplied is a positive one.

10. **G** In a supply curve, there is a positive relationship between price and quantity—as one increases, the other increases.

11. **D** Market equilibrium is reached when demand equals the quantity supplied.

12. **G** At 600 million, the supply and demand curves meet. The price at that point is $15.00.

13. **C** Following the Series 1 Curve, 900 million CDs are supplied at $15.00.

Lesson 6.2

Macroeconomics and Government Policy, p. 81

1. **C** Half of the United States government's revenue comes from income taxes.

2. **F** The government's budget deficit is the amount of revenue it must borrow to meet its financial obligations.

3. **C** When you buy a savings bond, you are loaning the government money to use on projects or services. After a certain amount of time, the government pays off its bonds with interest when they come due. Answers A, B, and D are examples of how the government collects revenue not of how it borrows funds.

4. **G** Government expenditures are money that is paid out by the government to conduct its business.

5. **B** The highest single category was $1435.2 billion for Medicare and Medicaid.

6. **H** The Defense ($744 billion) is almost equal to the Social Security ($730.1 billion) portion.

7 **A** If the federal deficit were to decrease, the government would pay less in interest because it would not owe as much money.

8. **A** Some tax policies are designed to influence the behavior of individuals or businesses; the other products would be taxed at a high rate to discourage smoking, drinking, and overuse of gasoline.

9. **B** Quotas limit imported goods and tariffs are taxes on imported goods; the administration of both can protect local businesses.

10. **G** Recent government subsidies have been given to the producers of dairy products, soybeans, wheat, and corn.

11. **B** New regulations can require companies to add steps to their production process, thereby increasing costs.

12. **H** The Federal Reserve's policies emphasize controlling inflation.

13. **B** Subsidies are payments to the producer or consumer of a local good or service, which results in lower cost of production and therefore a lower cost for consumers.

14. **H** The Federal Reserve works to preserve and maintain the financial stability of the United States.

15. **B** The Federal Reserve has many ways to increase or decrease the supply of money.

16. **G** Market failures occur as a result of imperfect competition and gaps between the private coast and the social cost of behaviors or actions.

17. **B** The Clayton Antitrust Act of 1914 outlawed price discrimination and enhanced competition.

Lesson 6.3

Macroeconomics, the GDP, and Price Fluctuation, p. 85

1. **D** Gross domestic product (GDP) is determined by multiplying final goods and services by their prices.

2. **F** Bartering is not counted in GDP, so the GDP of this nation would give an inaccurate picture of the strength of this nation's economy.

3. **B** GDP can count negative events as beneficial. Wars and natural disasters can raise GDP, however these events can have an overall negative effect on a nation.

4. **J** Final goods made in the United States and sold in the United States count toward United States GDP.

5. **C** The GDP of Mexico is 1.2 trillion and the GDP of the United Kingdom is twice that at 2.4 trillion.

6. **J** GDP is a quarterly measure and its changes every three months help economists identify economic trends.

7. **B** Inflation is a rise in the general level of prices over time.

8. **H** The same goods will cost $98.00.

9. **A** Prices fell between 1923 and 1933.

10. **G** If the 2013 price ($238) rose 2% by 2023, the price would be approximately $245.

11. **B** Unemployment appeared to reach a high of 10 percent at the end of 2009.

12. **F** Unemployment was close to 6 percent at the beginning of 2003 and close to 8 percent at the beginning of 2013.

Lesson 7.1

Major Economic Events, p. 89

1. **D** When prices increase, people buy less, which shrinks GDP and weakens the economy.

2. **F** Mass production of the Model T cut its price to 1/3 of the cost before mass production.

3. **C** A drop in supply when demand is high can lead to price increases.

4. **G** The economic boom of the Roaring Twenties was followed by one of the biggest busts in history.

5. **B** The sell-off in October 1929 was heightened when investors saw the value of their stocks fall and panicked, selling off their stocks, which caused the stocks to fall further.

6. **J** The Great Depression was so severe that it would have taken a long time for relief programs to help all of those who were poor and homeless.

7. **A** President Hoover presided over the government as the Great Depression worsened with no relief during the early 1930s.

8. **H** Building shantytowns on public or unused land would have been more acceptable to the authorities than building them on private land or in the middle of cities.

9. **C** Roosevelt's New Deal was intended to help stimulate the economy.

10. **G** Hoover believed that the policies of socialist governments in Europe worsened the Depression there and did not want to repeat that error.

11. **B** During the early 1930s, farmers destroyed their crops to reduce the supply, in hopes that increased demand would raise the prices.

12. **J** Through the AAA, farmers were paid to produce fewer crops, causing the price of agricultural products to increase.

13. **C** Social Security is a form of reliable assistance for all Americans.

14. **G** Roosevelt states that his primary task is to put people to work, but this can only be accomplished through government intervention.

Lesson 7.2

The Relationship Between Politics and Economics, p. 93

1. **D** The speech indicates that Coolidge wanted to reduce taxes and minimize legislation that would interfere with business and individual prosperity.

2. **H** Coolidge rejects the idea that the rich should be taxed more, and makes the point that those who are successful should not be punished for their success.

3. **A** Coolidge implies that it is unjust to tax rich people at a higher rate, and that they should not be punished for their prosperity. This indicates that Coolidge does not believe that the system helped certain people to become rich but that they earned it themselves.

4. **F** The New Deal used Keynesian economic ideas to intervene in the economy during the Great Depression.

5. **B** The country was producing more goods than Americans could buy.

6. **G** The destruction and instability caused by war can disrupt business and everyday life.

7. **C** A tariff is a tax on goods that are brought into a country to sell.

8. **F** Annexation is taking control of another country or territory, as the United States did with Hawaii in 1898.

9. **A** She states that the will of God made her heir apparent and the grace of God made her queen.

10. **J** The queen considers Hawaii to be an independent nation whose rule should be in the hands of chiefs.

11. **A** An increase in unemployment due to disruptions in businesses could cause homelessness.

12. **G** War and political instability frightens away investors.

13. **C** Humanitarian aid improves people's lives and reduces suffering.

14. **F**   Financial aid can provide economic stability, which can lead to political stability, which is in the best interest of US foreign policy.

Lesson 7.3

The Scientific and Industrial Revolutions, p. 97

1. **C**   The scientific method is the process used by scientists for testing ideas through experimentation and careful observation.

2. **J**   During the Scientific Revolution, rational thinking caused people to question old ideas about the world and look for new answers.

3. **A**   Antonie von Leeuwenhoek discovered cells in living matter through observation with a microscope.

4. **H**   The astrolabe allowed sailors to use the position of the sun and stars to determine the time of a celestial event, such as a sunrise or sunset.

5. **B**   The astrolabe helped make European exploration possible.

6. **H**   An industrial revolution shifts the economy from farming and trading to the manufacturing of goods.

7. **D**   Machines powered by water and steam needed to be housed in factories, rather than private homes or workshops.

8. **H**   As part of Britain's colonial empire, India sent tons of raw cotton to be used in England's cloth-making mills.

9. **B**   According to the table, cotton mills were concentrated in northwest England, so movement into cities was highest in that area of England.

10. **J**   In the first half of the 19th century, the development of railroads helped speed the development of the Industrial Revolution in England.

11. **A**   Since the southwest region contained only one factory, any goods produced there during this period were most likely the result of the old cottage industry system.

12. **F**   Industrialization affected farming, too, as new machines replaced farm workers. Factories in cities needed workers nearby.

13. **A**   Before labor unions, employers were free to treat workers according to their own company's rules.

14. **J**   Only the youngest children would likely be able to fit under running machines.

15. **C**   Poverty most likely forced families to send their children to work in factories.

Lesson 8.1

Savings and Banking, p. 101

1. **D**   An electronic funds transfer is another acceptable way to transfer money from banks.

2. **A**   Banks keep reserves of cash available to cover depositors' withdrawals.

3. **D**   Credit unions originally provided emergency loans to their members, who often were unable to get loans from other lenders.

4. **A**   In the past, different banks offered different types of services, but now most offer the same services.

5. **B**   Banks advertise that they have insurance to honor their promises to return deposits, if necessary.

6. **D** Savings and loan associations, like savings banks and credit unions, are thrift institutions.

7. **D** Having a personal checking account allows you to withdraw money, to use an ATM, to pay bills electronically, to use an ETF, and to write checks.

8. **C** Both the bank and the institution that received the check may charge a fee if you write a check for an amount greater than the account's balance.

9. **B** All banks are required to protect the privacy of their depositors.

10. **C** She is writing the check to Leadville Water Company.

11. **D** In order to be cashed or deposited, a check must be endorsed, or signed, by the check's recipient, the person to whom it is issued.

12. **B** Electronic transfers allow people with checking accounts the ability to set up automatic bill payments.

Lesson 8.2

Types of Consumer Credit, p. 105

1. **B** If the borrower defaults on a secured loan, the lender assumes the asset or property that secured the loan.

2. **H** Credit reports indicate if a person's identity has been stolen or used to purchase items illegally.

3. **A** If the interest on a secured loan such as a home equity loan is tax deductible, it can help reduce your taxes.

4. **G** Credit card companies make most of their money by charging fees and interest on debts they are owed.

5. **A** A credit score reflects how well someone pays his or her bills.

6. **H** Falling behind on loan or credit card payments can reduce a person's credit score.

7 **B** A drop in a person's credit score usually results in a more difficult time getting credit.

8. **G** Credit agencies get their information from banks and credit card companies.

9. **B** The finance charge is the amount you pay for credit.

10. **J** Because a car is a large purchase and would have to paid off over a period of time, buying a car on a credit card is not advisable because the interest rates are usually higher than those of other types of credit.

11. **D** High interest, declining property values, and an unreliable source of income should all be red flags to home buyers.

12. **F** Legally, you are allowed to obtain your credit report once each year for free from a reputable consumer credit reporting agency

13. **C** Interest is not charged on balances completely paid off each month.

14. **G** These types of purchases are usually made with secured loans.

15. **B** According to the information in the passage, credit card debt is becoming more of a problem with each passing generation.

16. **J** Younger people are carrying a balance and not paying off their purchases each month.

17. **B** This trend shows that credit card companies see a good potential market in younger customers.

18. **H** This amount is an increase of the same amount during the previous generation.

Lesson 8.3

Consumer Credit Laws, p. 109

1. **B**   The Fair Credit Reporting Act states that consumers have a right to have access to their credit reports.

2. **F**   The "Opt Out" provision states that consumers can choose to have their names removed from lender marketing lists.

3. **A**   The Truth in Lending Act limits a consumer's liability.

4. **J**   The Equal Credit Opportunity Act prohibits discrimination in credit transactions on the basis of certain personal characteristics.

5. **D**   The Consumer Credit Protection Act is an "umbrella" act that includes acts related to consumer credit protection.

6. **J**   The writer is questioning the effectiveness of the Credit CARD Act.

7. **A**   The writer believes that federal credit card protection has been inadequate to deal with the problems facing cardholders.

8. **H**   Credit card providers are prohibited from offering no-interest loans.

9. **D**   The APR is the most significant feature to compare credit card offers.

10. **H**   The CFPB is concerned with laws and regulations related to the sale of financial products and services.

11. **A**   The United States financial crisis that began in 2007 led to the creation of new regulations and laws as well as the creation of the CFPB.

12. **G**   Paying the balance due is the only way to avoid interest charges that are shown in the estimated payment column on the right.

13. **B**   The financial crisis of 2007 led to the creation of the Consumer Financial Protection Bureau through the Dodd-Frank Wall Street Reform and Consumer Protection Act.

14. **D**   The Credit CARD Act requires credit card providers to be consistent in payment dates and times.

Lesson 9.1

Development of Ancient Civilizations, p. 113

1. **D**   The Nile's annual floodwaters made agriculture possible, and this in turn gave rise to Egyptian civilization.

2. **G**   Most ancient civilizations developed near sources of water, such as rivers.

3. **A**   The delta is where the Nile empties into the Mediterranean Sea.

4. **J**   These pyramids reflect the ancient Egyptians' religious belief in an afterlife.

5. **C**   Both the Egyptian and Indian subcontinent civilizations were centered near rivers.

6. **F**   The economies of ancient Egypt and the Indus River Valley were dependent on agriculture.

7. **D**   The Aryans introduced the caste system, which divided society into four social classes.

8. **G**   A mandate is another word for *command.*

9. **A**   The Mandate of Heaven was a basic cultural belief for many centuries.

10. **H**   The Mandate of Heaven gave Chinese dynasties divine command, and the embodiment of the Egyptian ruler as the sun god gave the ruler the power of the divine

11. **A**   Unlike the governments of Egypt and China, the governments of Greece and Rome allowed ordinary citizens to participate.

12. **F**   In Rome, all male citizens were members of the Assembly of the People, which made laws, and in Athens, all male citizens could vote.

13. **C**   In a republic such as that of ancient Rome, elected representatives govern.

14. **J**   The geography of Greece isolated groups of people, giving rise to independent city-states.

15. **A**   Greek city-states were established with a hill at the center of each.

Lesson 9.2

Nationhood and Statehood, p. 117

1. **C**   The Mediterranean Sea and the Red Sea are physical boundaries because they are natural features that separate two regions from one another.

2. **H**   Mali is bordered by Mauritania, Algeria, Burkina Faso, Niger, Ivory Coast, Guinea, and Senegal.

3. **C**   Africa and Europe are separated from North and South America by the Atlantic Ocean.

4. **J**   The Rio Grande is a physical boundary because it forms a natural border between the United States and Mexico.

5. **C**   The Pacific Ocean serves as a border for Hawaii, Alaska, Washington, Oregon, and California.

6. **J**   The borders of ten states occur at the Mississippi River.

7. **A**   The degrees of lines of latitude decrease from north to south.

8. **H**   The border between Alaska and Canada follows a line of longitude.

9. **D**   The creation of new borders signified that Kazakhstan had become an independent nation.

10. **J**   The borders of the Soviet Union changed in 1991 when it was dissolved through negotiation.

Lesson 9.3

Human Activity and the Environment, p. 121

1. **D**   The president wants to develop renewable sources of energy, such as wind and solar energy.

2. **H**   The United States needs new sources of energy to meet the demands of its growing population.

3. **A**   Sustainable development encourages the use of renewable energy sources.

4. **F**   Nonrenewable refers to resources that cannot be replaced or that take a very long time to replace.

5. **A**   Because industries were less active following World War I, there were fewer greenhouse gas emissions, which led to lower temperatures.

6. **J**   Industry was less active during World War I, the Great Depression, and World War II, so there were fewer greenhouse gas emissions.

7. **A**   Droughts and floods change how much water is available to a community at any given time.

8. **H**   Natural gas, coal, and oil result from decaying carbon matter, usually under pressure.

9. **D**   Sustainable development advocates urge people to reduce consumption of natural resources, like oil and gas.

10. **G**   When consumers buy more fuel-efficient cars, increasing demand, automakers will produce more.

11. D As the standard of living improves around the world, people are consuming more electricity, gas, and energy to meet their needs.

12. H The biggest motivator for car manufacturer's is profit, which comes from an increase in consumer demand.

Lesson 10.1

Concepts of Region and Place, p. 125

1. D Both plains and plateaus are large flat areas, but a plateau rises higher than its surrounding areas, whereas a plain does not.

2. H These are all found within a grassland.

3. B Due to the harsh cold, dry climate of Antarctica, there is only one biome.

4. G All living organisms on Earth live on the layer known as the crust.

5. A The outer core is made of liquid metal, and the inner core is made of solid metal.

6. G The Earth's thickest layer, its mantle, is made of solid rock.

7. D North and South America have three countries that are among the world's leading producers.

8. F Chile produces more copper than the next three highest producers combined, but not as much as the next six highest producers combined.

9. A A tundra is cold for most of the year, so it would more likely occur in the Arctic.

10. F Biomes are regions that contain many similar ecosystems.

11. A Areas closest to the Equator have a more tropical climate than those farthest from it.

12. F The desert is almost half the size of Australia.

13. D The largest impact on temperature is from elevation, distance from the Equator, and distance from a large body of water.

Lesson 10.2

Natural and Cultural Diversity, p. 129

1. B The South Pole, the southern most point on Earth, is in Antarctica.

2. J All five bodies make up a continuous global ocean.

3. C Surrounded by mountains, the interior of Australia would be blocked from receiving any significant rainfall.

4. F The Arctic Circle has a cold, dry climate, which leads to a low density of plant and animal life.

5. D Diversity is defined as variety.

6. H Mandarin is the most commonly spoken language in the world.

7. C English, French, Italian, Greek and Sanskrit make up the Indo-European language family.

8. J Large numbers of Germans, English, Africans, and Irish migrated to America between 1607 and 1820.

9. B Bison are grazing animals, and as the Great Plains is grassland, the Lakota would have included bison in their diet.

10. J   People choose to settle in river valleys where flat land and access to water made farming and fishing easier. The rivers also provided a source of transportation.

11. C   The sparse populations of many Western states are a result of their extreme weather conditions.

12. F   Lakes and Oceans provide transportation, fishing, and tourism.

Lesson 10.3

Population Trends and Issues, p. 133

1. D   Population growth was high in the southwest, so there is probably a need for increased government services there.

2. G   Georgia was the fastest growing eastern state in population in this period.

3. B   Generally a high fertility rate and low mortality rate means a growing population.

4. G   The government uses census data in part to determine where new government services might be needed.

5. A   The map shows Japanese migration from East Asia to North America and South America.

6. J   Many Europeans migrated to North America to avoid war, food shortages, and religious and political persecution.

7. B   Mexico and Asia were the areas of origin for large migrations to the US.

8. J   These are part of the Buffalo Metropolitan Area.

9. C   Buffalo presents an example of urban sprawl because its urban areas have spread into the outlying areas.

10. J   1980–2010 is the period in which residential areas and businesses moved into outlying areas.

11. C   1950–1980 is the period that many city dwellers moved to the suburbs just outside the cities.